U.S. Department
of Transportation

**Federal Aviation
Administration**

)

ATP

# Airline Transport Pilot and Aircraft Type Rating

# Practical Test Standards

## for

## Airplane

# July 2008

Flight Standards Service
Washington, DC 20591

*(this page intentionally left blank)*

# Airline Transport Pilot and Aircraft Type Rating

# Practical Test Standards

## for

## Airplane

# 2008

Flight Standards Service
Washington, DC 20591

FAA-S-8081-5F

## Note

Material in FAA-S-8081-5F will be effective July 1, 2008. All previous editions of the Airline Transport Pilot and Aircraft Type Rating—Airplane Practical Test Standards will be obsolete as of this date.

*(this page intentionally left blank)*

## Record of Changes

### Change 1 (12/16/2008)

- Changes made to satisfy FAA Safety Recommendation 05.124.
- Added Elements 12 through 14 to "Special Emphasis Areas" in Introduction.
- Added Element 8 to Area of Operation I ("Preflight Preparation"), Task B ("Performance and Limitations").

### Change 2 (3/18/2009)

- Renumbered Objectives under Area of Operation I ("Preflight Preparation"), Task B ("Performance and Limitations").
- Changed AC 120-45 reference to reflect the replacement AC 61-136 in Appendix 1

### Change 3 (2/10/2011)

- Added English Language proficiency requirements.

### Change 4 (4/4/2012)

- Introduction
    - o Updated FSIMS website URL in "Practical Test Standards Concept" section
    - o Updated list of references.
    - o Revised Element 7 under "Special Emphasis Areas" to cover hot spots and NOTAMs.
    - o Added borders to Area of Operation 1 (Preflight Preparation), Task B (Performance and Limitations) to indicate Change 1.
    - o Revised paragraph 4 of the "Aircraft and Equipment Required for the Practical Test" section to cover meanings and limitations of airport taxiway, and runway signs, lights and markings.
    - o Revised paragraph 2 of the "Examiner Responsibility" section to add the requirement to include meanings and limitations of airport taxiway, and runway signs, lights and markings to examiner responsibility.

- Section 1: "Preflight Preparation"
    - o Revised and renumbered Area of Operation I ("Preflight Preparation"), Task B ("Performance Limitations"), Objective 2 to include departure and arrival airports, taxiways, and runways NOTAMs, runway usable lengths, hot spots, taxi restrictions, specific taxi procedures, as applicable, and signage/markings.

- Section 2: "Preflight Procedures, Inflight Maneuvers, and Postflight Procedures"
  - o Revised and renumbered Area of Operation II ("Preflight Procedures"), Task C ("Taxiing"), to add elements regarding taxiing demonstration requirements.
  - o Updated Area of Operation III ("Takeoff and Departure Phase"), Task F ("Powerplant Failure During Takeoff") Note.
  - o Updated Area of Operation IV ("Inflight Maneuvers"), Task B ("Approaches to Stalls and Stall Recovery") title, added 3 Notes, and updated elements 1, 2, 4, 5, and 6.
  - o Revised Area of Operation IV ("Inflight Maneuvers"), Task C ("Powerplant Failure – Multiengine Airplane") Note.
  - o Added Note to Area of Operation V ("Instrument Procedures"), Task C ("Precision Approaches (PA)").
  - o Revised Area of Operation VI ("Landings and Approaches to Landings") Note.
  - o Added 11 elements to Area of Operation IX ("Postflight Procedures"), Task A ("After-Landing Procedures"), Objective and renumbered all elements accordingly.
- Appendix – Airplanes Task vs. Simulation Device Credit
  - o Revised activity number 1
  - o Removed Flight Simulation Device levels 1, 2, and 3

## Change 5 (6/25/2013)

- Revised the *Removal of the "Limited to Center Thrust" Limitation* section of the Introduction (page 13).
  - o Changed the section title to *Removal of the "Limited to Center Thrust" Limitation or Initial ATP type rating Airplane Multiengine Class Certificate*
  - o Revised the first paragraph to clarify the requirements of 14 CFR part 61, section 61.153(d)(2).

## Change 6 (9/30/2013)

- Added Risk Management Handbook, FAA-H-8083-2 to reference list in *Practical Test Book Description* section of the Introduction (page 4).
  - o This guidance will assist the applicant and examiner on the "aeronautical decision making (ADM) / risk management" special emphasis area to be applied throughout the practical test.
- Revised the Removal of the "Limited to Center Thrust" Limitation section of the Introduction (page 13).

o  This change will allow those who hold an ATP or commercial license (with appropriate ratings) issued by a foreign Civil Aviation Authority to use that license as a basis for applying for an FAA issued ATP certificate or aircraft type rating. A restriction on the use of these foreign licenses was inadvertently created in Change 5 to this document on 6/25/2013.

## Change 7 (7/2/2014) – effective 8/1/2014

- Revised "Practical Test Prerequisites: Airline Transport Pilot" section in Introduction to incorporate new guidance for ATP Multiengine class certification and Multiengine type ratings (pages 9 through 12)

*(this page intentionally left blank)*

# Major Enhancements to Version FAA-S-8081-5F

- Corrected web addresses (URLs).
- Updated and added references.
- Added icing conditions and hazard awareness references, emphasis, and evaluation elements.
- Clarified multiengine requirements and results.
- Clarified possible results if applicant refuses to perform a task or element.
- Added traffic awareness to special emphasis area.
- Clarified when a medical certificate is required.
- Clarified requirement for inflight shutdown, feathering, if propeller-driven, and restart while airborne.
- Standardized "knowledge" terminology.
- Added single pilot resource management (SRM).
- Clarified intent for checklist accomplishment in crew-served airplanes.
- Added "Naval Vessel Protection" and "No Wake" zones in seaplane area.
- Added "Applicant Notes:" to clarify intent, scope, and range of the examiner's authorization to conduct the evaluation.
- Added "bank" to unusual attitudes for clarification.
- Added "displays" to tasks where appropriate to include evaluation of newer avionics and usage of panel multifunction displays.
- Clarified intent for raw data approaches to be flown as much as possible by reference to standby or backup instrumentation.
- Revised verbiage to allow "approved method" in addition to manufacturer's method concerning checklist performance.

*(this page intentionally left blank)*

# Foreword

The Airline Transport Pilot and Aircraft Type Rating—Airplane Practical Test Standards (PTS) book has been published by the Federal Aviation Administration (FAA) to establish the standards for airline transport pilot and aircraft type rating practical tests for airplanes. FAA inspectors, designated pilot examiners, and check airmen (referred to as examiners throughout the remaining practical test standard) must conduct practical tests in compliance with these standards. Flight instructors and applicants should find these standards helpful in practical test preparation.

---

Joseph K. Tintera, Manager
Regulatory Support Division, AFS-600
Flight Standards Service

*(this page intentionally left blank)*

# Table of Contents

## Introduction

General Information ................................................................ 1

Practical Test Standards Concept ...................................... 1

Practical Test Book Description ......................................... 2

Abbreviations ......................................................................... 6

Use of the Practical Test Standards ................................. 7

Special Emphasis Areas ...................................................... 9

Practical Test Prerequisites:  Airline Transport Pilot
Multiengine Class (14 CFR part 61, section 61.159) .............. 9

Practical Test Prerequisites:  Airline Transport Pilot
Multiengine Class with Restricted Privileges (14 CFR part
61, section 61.160) ................................................................ 10

Practical Test Prerequisites:  Aircraft Type Rating ..................... 13

Aircraft Type Ratings Limited to "VFR Only" .............................. 14

Removal of the "Limited to Center Thrust" Limitation or
Initial ATP/type rating Airplane Multiengine Class
Certificate ............................................................................. 15

Aircraft and Equipment Required for the Practical Test ............ 16

Use of an FAA-Approved Flight Simulator or Flight Training
Device .................................................................................... 17

Examiner Responsibility ................................................................ 18

Satisfactory Performance .............................................................. 19

Unsatisfactory Performance ......................................................... 20

Letter of Discontinuance .............................................................. 21

Aeronautical Decision Making (ADM) and Risk Management ... 21

Crew Resource Management (CRM and Single Pilot Resource
Management (SRM)) ............................................................. 21

How the Examiner Evaluates CRM/SRM .................................... 22

Applicant's Use of Checklists ....................................................... 23

Use of Distractions during Practical Tests ................................. 23

Positive Exchange of Flight Controls .......................................... 23

## Section 1: Preflight Preparation

## Areas of Operation

I.    Preflight Preparation ............................................................. 27

      Task A:   Equipment Examination ......................................... 27

Task B:  Performance and Limitations..............................28

Task C: Water and Seaplane Characteristics
        (AMES/ASES) ........................................................30

Task D:  Seaplane Bases, Maritime Rules, and Aids
        to Marine Navigation (AMES/ASES)......................30

**Section 2: Preflight Procedures, Inflight Maneuvers, and Postflight Procedures**

**Areas of Operation**

II.  Preflight Procedures ...........................................................35

    Task A:  Preflight Inspection.................................................35
    Task B:  Powerplant Start.....................................................37
    Task C:  TAXIING ................................................................37
    Task D:  Sailing (AMES/ASES)..............................................38
    Task E:  Seaplane Base/Water Landing Site
            Markings and Lighting (AMES, ASES) ...................38
    Task F:  Pre-Takeoff Checks ...............................................39

III.  Takeoff and Departure Phase............................................40

    Task A:  Normal and Crosswind Takeoff..............................40
    Task B:  Glassy Water Takeoff and Climb
            (AMES/ASES) ........................................................41
    Task C:  Rough Water Takeoff and Climb
            (AMES/ASES) ........................................................41
    Task D:  Confined-Area Takeoff and Climb
            (AMES/ASES) ........................................................42
    Task E:  Instrument Takeoff ...............................................43
    Task F:  Powerplant Failure during Takeoff .......................45
    Task G:  Rejected Takeoff ...................................................46
    Task H:  Departure Procedures ..........................................47

IV.  Inflight Maneuvers .............................................................49

    Task A:  Steep Turns ............................................................49
    Task B:  Approaches to Stalls and Stall Recovery...............49
    Task C:  Powerplant Failure—Multiengine Airplane ..........51
    Task D:  Powerplant Failure—Single–Engine
            Airplane.................................................................52
    Task E:  Specific Flight Characteristics ...............................53
    Task F:  Recovery from Unusual Attitudes..........................53

V.  Instrument Procedures.............................................54

    Task A:  Standard Terminal Arrival/Flight
            Management System Procedures.........................54
    Task B:  Holding.............................................................55
    Task C:  Precision Approaches (PA)................................56
    Task D:  Nonprecision Approaches (NPA) ..................58
    Task E:  Circling Approach............................................59
    Task F:  Missed Approach ............................................60

VI. Landings and Approaches to Landings .................62

    Task A:  Normal and Crosswind Approaches and
            Landings ........................................................62
    Task B:  Landing from a Precision Approach......................63
    Task C:  Approach and Landing with (Simulated)
            Powerplant Failure—Multiengine Airplane..........64
    Task D:  Landing From a Circling Approach ......................65
    Task E:  Rough Water Approach and Landing
            (AMES/ASES).................................................66
    Task F:  Glassy Water Approach And Landing
            (AMES/ASES).................................................67
    Task G:  Confined-Area Approach and Landing
            (AMES/ASES).................................................68
    Task H:  Rejected Landing.............................................69
    Task I:  Landing from a No Flap or a Nonstandard
            Flap Approach ...............................................69

VII. Normal and Abnormal Procedures.........................71

    Task A:  Normal and Abnormal Procedures .................71

VIII. Emergency Procedures...........................................72

    Task A:  Emergency Procedures .................................72

IX. Postflight Procedures ..........................................73

    Task A:  After-Landing Procedures..............................73
    Task B:  Anchoring (AMES/ASES) ..............................74
    Task C:  Docking and Mooring (AMES/ASES) ..............74
    Task D:  Beaching (AMES/ASES) ................................74
    Task E:  Ramping (AMES/ASES)..................................75
    Task F:  Parking and Securing ....................................75

# Appendix: Task vs. Simulation Device Credit

Task vs. Simulation Device Credit ............................................. 77
Use of Chart ...................................................................... 77
Task vs. Simulation Device Credit ............................................. 78
Task vs. Simulation Device Credit ............................................. 79
Task vs. Simulation Device Credit ............................................. 80

# Introduction

## General Information

The Flight Standards Service of the Federal Aviation Administration (FAA) has developed this practical test standard (PTS) to be used by examiners[1] when conducting airline transport pilot and aircraft type rating practical tests in airplanes. Instructors are expected to address all of the elements contained in this PTS when preparing applicants for practical tests. Applicants should be familiar with this PTS and refer to these standards during their training.

The FAA gratefully acknowledges the valuable assistance provided by many individuals, companies, and organizations throughout the aviation community who have contributed their time and talent in assisting with the development of this practical test standard.

This PTS may be purchased from the Superintendent of Documents, U.S. Government Printing Office (GPO), Washington, DC 20402-9325, or from GPO's web site at: http://bookstore.gpo.gov

This PTS is also available for download, in pdf format, from www.faa.gov

This PTS is published by the U.S. Department of Transportation, Federal Aviation Administration, Airman Testing Standards Branch, AFS-630, P.O. Box 25082, Oklahoma City, OK 73125.

Comments regarding this publication may be emailed to AFS630comments@faa.gov.

## Practical Test Standards Concept

Title 14 of the Code of Federal Regulations (14 CFR) part 61 specifies the areas in which knowledge and skill must be demonstrated by the applicant before the issuance of an airline transport pilot certificate and/ or a type rating in airplanes. The CFRs provide the flexibility to permit the FAA to publish practical test standards containing the Areas of Operation and specific Tasks in which pilot competency must be demonstrated. Title 49 of the U.S. Code (Transportation) requires the administrator to promulgate rules and set standards in the interest of public safety.

---

[1] The word "examiner" denotes either the FAA inspector, FAA designated pilot examiner, or other authorized person who conducts the practical test.

**Adherence to provisions of the regulations and the PTS is mandatory for the evaluation of airline transport pilot and type rating applicants.** For some aircraft types, however, provisions of FAA Flight Standardization Board (FSB) Reports may specify special details as to how 14 CFR part 61 and this PTS apply to certain maneuvers, Tasks, procedures, or knowledge areas. FSB Reports are available from the Flight Standards Service System Safety's web site at: http://fsims.faa.gov.

*NOTE: Pilots employed by an air carrier certificate holder, operating under 14 CFR part 121 or 135, or as authorized by the Administrator, whose manual prohibits a circling approach when the weather is below 1,000 feet and 3 miles' visibility, are not required to be checked on the circling approach and landing from a circling approach. Aircraft type ratings added to an airline transport pilot certificate issued without training and checking in the circling maneuver, as authorized, will be annotated "MD-11 CIRC. APCH-VMC ONLY," for example. This restriction may be removed when the circling approach is satisfactorily demonstrated to a designated examiner, a check airman who is a designated examiner, or an FAA inspector, in the appropriate type airplane. If, under 14 CFR part 121 or 135, or as authorized by the Administrator, the initial airline transport pilot certificate is issued coincident with a type rating, with a circling approach restriction, the airline transport pilot certificate will be annotated, "ATP CIRC. APCH-VMC ONLY, MD-11 CIRC. APCH-VMC ONLY," for example. This restriction to the airline transport pilot certificate level will be removed when the first unrestricted airline transport pilot certificate or airline transport pilot type rating is issued. The respective circling approach restriction will then be annotated on the certificate, as listed in the first example.*

## Practical Test Book Description

This practical test book contains the Airline Transport Pilot and Aircraft Type Rating Practical Test Standards—Airplane.

The Airline Transport Pilot and Aircraft Type Rating Practical Test Standards—Airplane includes Areas of Operation and Tasks for the initial issuance of an airline transport pilot certificate and for the addition of category, class, and aircraft type ratings to an airline transport pilot certificate. These Areas of Operation and Tasks also apply for the issuance of an airplane type rating to a private or commercial pilot certificate.

The Areas of Operation are divided into two sections. The first Area of Operation in each section is conducted on the ground to determine the applicant's knowledge of the aircraft, equipment, performance, and limitations.

The eight Areas of Operation located in the second section, numbered II-IX, are considered to be the flight portion of the practical test. All eight of these Areas of Operation test the applicant's knowledge and skills.

If all Tasks of the practical test are not completed on one date, all remaining Tasks of the test must be satisfactorily completed not more than 60 calendar days after the date on which the applicant began the test.

**Areas of Operation** are phases of the practical test arranged in a logical sequence within each standard. They begin with Preflight Preparation and end with Postflight Procedures. The examiner may combine Tasks with similar objectives and conduct the practical test in any sequence that will result in a complete and efficient test; **however, the ground portion of the practical test must be accomplished before the flight portion.**

**Tasks** are titles of knowledge areas, flight procedures, or maneuvers appropriate to an Area of Operation.

**References** identify the publication(s) that describe(s) the. Descriptions of specific Tasks are not included in the practical test standards because this information can be found in the current issue of the listed references. Publications other than those listed may be used for references if their content conveys substantially the same meaning as the referenced publications.

This practical test standard is based on the following references:

| | |
|---|---|
| **Public Law 110-135** | Dated 12-12-2007 |
| **14 CFR part 1** | Definitions and Abbreviations |
| **14 CFR parts 23/25** | Airworthiness Standards |
| **14 CFR part 61** | Certification: Pilots, Flight Instructors, and Ground Instructors |
| **14 CFR part 71** | Designation of Class A, B, C, D, and E Airspace Areas; Airways; Air Traffic Service; Routes; and Reporting points |
| **14 CFR part 91** | General Operating and Flight Rules |
| **14 CFR part 121** | Operating Requirements: Domestic, flag, and Supplemental Operations |

**Change 4 (4/4/2012) and Change 6 (9/30/2013)**

| | |
|---|---|
| **14 CFR part 135** | Operating Requirements: Commuter and On Demand Operations and Rules Governing Persons on Board Such Aircraft |

| | |
|---|---|
| **14 CFR part 139**<br>**49 CFR part 830** | Certification and Operations:<br>Notification and Reporting of Aircraft<br>Accidents or Incidents and Overdue<br>Aircraft, and Preservation of Aircraft<br>Wreckage, Mail, Cargo, and Records |
| **FAA-H-8083-1** | Aircraft Weight and Balance<br>Handbook |
| **FAA-H-8083-2** | Risk Management Handbook |
| **FAA-H-8083-3** | Airplane Flying Handbook |
| **FAA-H-8083-15** | Instrument Flying Handbook |
| **FAA-H-8083-23** | Seaplane, Skiplane, and Float/Ski<br>Equipped Helicopter Operations Book |
| **FAA-H-8083-25** | Pilot's Handbook of Aeronautical<br>Knowledge |
| **FAA-H-8261-1** | Instrument Procedures Handbook |
| **AC 00-2** | Advisory Circular Checklist |
| **AC 00-6** | Aviation Weather |
| **AC 00-45** | Aviation Weather Services |
| **AC 20-29** | Use of Aircraft Fuel Anti-icing<br>Additives |
| **AC 20-117** | Hazards Following Ground Deicing<br>and Ground Operations in Conditions<br>Conducive to Aircraft Icing<br>Aeronautical Decision Making |
| **AC 60-22** | Aeronautical Decision Making |
| **AC 60-28** | English Language Skill Standards<br>Required by 14 CFR parts 61, 63, and<br>65 |
| **AC 61-84** | Role of Preflight Preparation |
| **AC 61-134** | General Aviation Controlled flight into<br>Terrain Awareness |
| **AC 61-136** | FAA Approval of Basic Aviation<br>Training Devices (BATD) and<br>Advanced Aviation Training Devices<br>(AATD) |
| **AC 90-79** | Recommended Practices and<br>Procedures for the Use of Long-<br>Range Navigation |
| **AC 90-91** | North American Route Program<br>(NRP) |

| | |
|---|---|
| AC 90-94 | Guidelines for Using Global Positioning System Equipment for Non Precision Instrument Approaches in the U.S. National Airspace system |
| AC 90-100 | U.S. Terminal and En Route Area Navigation (RNAV) Operations |
| AC 91-43 | Unreliable Airspeed Indications |
| AC 91-51 | Effect of Icing on Aircraft Control and Airplane Deice and Anti-ice Systems |
| AC 91-70 | Oceanic Operations |
| AC 91-73 | Part 91 and Part 135 Single-Pilot Procedures During Taxi Operations |
| AC 91-74 | Pilot Guide—Flight in Icing Conditions |
| AC 91-79 | Runway Overrun Prevention |
| AC 120-27 | Aircraft Weight and Balance Control |
| AC 120-28 | Criteria for Approval of Category III Landing Weather Minima for Takeoff, Landing, and Rollout |
| AC 120-29 | Criteria for Approval of Category I and Category II Weather Minima for Approach |
| AC 120-51 | Crew Resource Management Training |
| AC 120-57 | Surface Movement Guidance System |
| AC 120-60 | Ground Deicing and Anti-icing Program |
| AC 120-62 | Takeoff Safety Training Aid |
| AC 120-74 | Parts 91, 121, 125, and 135 Flightcrew Procedures During Taxi Operations |
| AC 135-17 | Pilot Guide—Small Aircraft Ground Deicing |
| AC 150-5340-18 | Standards for Airport Sign Systems |
| AFD | Airport Facility Directory |
| AFM | FAA-Approved Airplane Flight Manual |
| AIM | Aeronautical Information Manual |
| CDL | Configuration Deviation List |
| DP | Departure Procedures |
| FDC NOTAM | National Flight Data Center Notices to Airmen |
| FSB Reports | Flight Standardization Board Reports |
| IAP | Instrument Approach Procedure |
| IFIM | International Flight Information Manual |
| MEL | Minimum Equipment List |
| NOTAM | Notices to Airmen |
| ODP | Obstacle Departure Procedure |

| | |
|---|---|
| **Other** | En Route Low and High Altitude Charts, Profile Descent Charts, Pertinent Pilot's Operating Handbooks, and Flight Manuals |
| **SIAP** | Standard Instrument Approach Procedure Charts |
| **STAR** | Standard Terminal Arrival |

*NOTE:* *The latest revision of these references should be used.*

**Objectives** list the important elements that must be satisfactorily performed to demonstrate competency in a Task. Objectives include:

1. specifically what the applicant should be able to do,
2. the conditions under which the Task is to be performed, and
3. the acceptable standards of performance.

**Notes** are used to emphasize special considerations required in the Areas of Operation or Tasks.

### Abbreviations

| | |
|---|---|
| **14 CFR** | Title 14 of the Code of Federal Regulations |
| **AC** | Advisory Circular |
| **ADM** | Aeronautical Decision Making |
| **AGL** | Above Ground Level |
| **AMEL** | Airplane Multiengine Land |
| **AMES** | Airplane Multiengine Sea |
| **ATC** | Air Traffic Control |
| **CDL** | Configuration Deviation List |
| **CFIT** | Controlled Flight into Terrain |
| **CRM** | Crew Resource Management |
| **DA** | Decision Altitude |
| **DH** | Decision Height |
| **DP** | Departure Procedure |
| **FAA** | Federal Aviation Administration |
| **FAF** | Final Approach Fix |
| **FDC** | Flight Data Center |
| **FE** | Flight Engineer |
| **FMS** | Flight Management System |
| **FMSP** | Flight Management System Procedures |
| **FSB** | Flight Standardization Board |
| **FSD** | Flight Simulation Device |
| **FSDO** | Flight Standards District Office |
| **FTD** | Flight Training Device |
| **GLS** | GNSS Landing System |
| **GNSS** | Global Navigation Satellite System |
| **GPO** | Government Printing Office |

| | |
|---|---|
| GPS | Global Positioning System |
| IAP | Instrument Approach Procedure |
| IFR | Instrument Flight Rules |
| ILS | Instrument Landing System |
| INS | Inertial Navigation System |
| LAHSO | Land and Hold Short Operations |
| LDA | Localizer-type Directional Aid |
| LOC | ILS Localizer |
| MDA | Minimum Descent Altitude |
| MEL | Minimum Equipment List |
| NAVAID | Navigation Aid |
| NDB | Non-directional Beacon |
| NOTAM | Notice to Airmen |
| NWS | National Weather Service |
| POH | Pilot's Operating Handbook |
| PT | Procedure Turn |
| PTS | Practical Test Standard |
| RNAV | Area Navigation |
| SRM | Single-Pilot Resource Management |
| STAR | Standard Terminal Arrival |
| TAA | Terminal Arrival Area |
| V1 | Takeoff Decision Speed |
| V2 | Takeoff Safety Speed |
| VDP | Visual Descent Point |
| VFR | Visual Flight Rules |
| $V_{MC}$ | Minimum Control Speed with Critical Engine Inoperative |
| VMC | Visual Meteorological Conditions |
| VOR | Very High Frequency Ominidirectional Range |
| VR | Rotation Speed |
| VREF | Reference Landing Approach Speed |
| VSSE | Safe, Intentional, One-Engine Inoperative Speed |
| $V_X$ | Best Angle of Climb Speed |
| $V_Y$ | Best Rate of Climb Speed |

### *Use of the Practical Test Standards*

The Tasks in this PTS are for an initial airline transport pilot certificate, or the addition of a category, class, or aircraft type rating to an airline transport pilot certificate. All appropriate Tasks required for an initial type rating are also required for pilot-in-command proficiency checks conducted in accordance with 14 CFR part 61, section 61.58.

**All Tasks are required,** except as noted. When a particular element **is not appropriate to the aircraft or its equipment,** that element may be omitted.

If the multiengine airplane used for the flight check does not publish a $V_{MC}$, then the "Limited to Centerline Thrust" restriction will be added to any certificate issued from this check, unless competence in a multiengine airplane with a published $V_{MC}$ has already been demonstrated.

Examples of element exceptions are: integrated flight systems for aircraft not so equipped, operation of landing gear in fixed gear aircraft, multiengine Tasks in single-engine aircraft, or other situations where the aircraft operation is not compatible with the requirement of the element.

If an applicant refuses to demonstrate a requested maneuver, the examiner may issue a Letter of Discontinuance to allow the examiner and applicant to discuss the applicant's concern about the requested maneuver, or a Notice of Disapproval, if the examiner determines the applicant's skill and abilities to be in serious doubt.

In preparation for each practical test, the examiner shall develop a written "plan of action" for each practical test. The "plan of action" is a tool, for the sole use of the examiner, to be used in evaluating the applicant. The plan of action need not be grammatically correct or in any formal format. The plan of action must contain all of the required Areas of Operation and Tasks and any optional Tasks selected by the examiner.

The "plan of action" shall incorporate one or more scenarios that will be used during the practical test. The examiner should try to include as many of the Tasks into the scenario portion of the test as possible, but maintain the flexibility to change due to unexpected situations as they arise and still result in an efficient and valid test. *Any Task selected for evaluation during a practical test shall be evaluated in its entirety.*

NOTE:   *Any equipment inoperative in accordance with a minimum equipment list (MEL) shall be placarded in accordance with the approved MEL procedures and explained by the applicant to the examiner describing the procedures accomplished, the resulting operational restrictions, and the documentation for the item(s).*

## Special Emphasis Areas

Examiners must place special emphasis upon areas of aircraft operations considered critical to flight safety. Among these are:

1. positive aircraft control
2. procedures for positive exchange of flight controls
3. stall/spin awareness
4. special use airspace and other airspace areas
5. collision avoidance procedures
6. wake turbulence and low level wind shear avoidance procedures
7. runway incursion avoidance and good cockpit discipline during taxi operations, hot spots, and NOTAMs
8. land and hold short operations (LAHSO)
9. controlled flight into terrain (CFIT)
10. aeronautical decision making (ADM)/risk management; and
11. crew resource management/single-pilot resource management (CRM/SRM) to include automation management
12. recognition of wing contamination to icing
13. adverse effects of wing contamination in icing conditions during takeoff, cruise, and landing phases of flight
14. icing procedures of information published by the manufacturer, within the AFM, that is specific to the type of aircraft
15. traffic awareness, "See and Avoid" concept

Although these areas may not be specifically addressed under each Task, they are essential to flight safety and will be critically evaluated during the practical test. In all instances, the applicant's actions must relate to the complete situation.

Prior to the test, the examiner must explain, and the applicant must understand, the examiner's role regarding air traffic control (ATC), crew resource management (CRM), and the duties and responsibilities of the examiner through all phases of the practical test.

### Practical Test Prerequisites: Airline Transport Pilot Multiengine Class (14 CFR part 61, section 61.159)

An applicant for the original issuance of an airline transport pilot certificate in the airplane category multiengine class rating is required (prior to taking the practical test) by 14 CFR part 61 to:

1. have passed the ATP (ARA, ATA or ATP test codes) aeronautical knowledge test within 24 calendar months of the practical test and present an unexpired Computer Test Report (ARA, ATA, or ATP coded tests are not valid if

expired, even for air carrier flight crewmembers after July 31, 2014) or

2.  have passed the ATP Multiengine Class aeronautical knowledge test (test code ATM) after July 31, 2014 within 60 calendar months before the date of the practical test except for employees of (or employed by):

    a.  flight crewmembers employed by part 119 certificate holders and that have passed the operator's approved pilot-in-command training or checking program,

    b.  a flight crew member for a part 119 certificate holder operating under part 121 at the time of the practical test and has satisfactorily completed the operator's initial training program, or

    c.  by the U.S. Armed Forces as a flight crew member at the time of the practical test in U.S. military air transport operations and has completed the pilot-in-command aircraft qualification training program appropriate to the pilot certificate and rating sought.

**Note:** *Applicants qualified by a, b, or c qualify for the practical test with an expired knowledge test if it was passed after July 31, 2014. Applicants must present a graduation certificate for completion of an ATP certification training program with any ATP (ATM test code) knowledge test results dated after July 31, 2014.*

3.  have the aeronautical experience prescribed in 14 CFR part 61, section 61.159, that applies to the aircraft category and class rating

4.  have a minimum of a third-class medical certificate, if a medical certificate is required (if any portion of the certification must occur in an actual airplane, then a medical certificate is required for that portion)

5.  be at least 23 years of age

6.  be able to read, speak, write, and understand the English language. If there is any doubt, consult AC 60-28, English Language Skill Standards Required by 14 CFR parts 61, 63, and 65, or contact your local Flight Standards District Office (FSDO). The examiner must determine whether the applicant meets the English language requirements before beginning the practical test.

## Practical Test Prerequisites: Airline Transport Pilot Multiengine Class with Restricted Privileges (14 CFR part 61, section 61.160)

An applicant for the original issuance of an airline transport pilot certificate with an airplane category multiengine class rating after

July 31, 2014 is required (prior to taking the practical test) by 14 CFR part 61 to:

1. have passed the ATP (ARA, ATA or ATP test codes) aeronautical knowledge test within 24 calendar months of the practical test and present an unexpired Computer Test Report or

2. have passed the ATP Multiengine Class aeronautical knowledge test appropriate airline transport pilot knowledge test (test code "ATM") within 60 calendar months before the date of the practical test  except for employees of (or employed by):

    a. flight crewmembers employed by part 119 certificate holders  and that have passed the operator's approved pilot-in-command training or checking program,

    b. a flight crew member for a part 119 certificate holder operating under part 121 at the time of the practical test and has satisfactorily completed the operator's initial training program, or

    c. by the U.S. Armed Forces as a flight crew member at the time of the practical test in U.S. military air transport operations  and has completed the pilot-in-command aircraft qualification training program appropriate to the pilot certificate and rating sought.

**NOTE:** *Applicants qualified by a, b, or  c qualify for the practical test with an expired knowledge test if it was passed after July 31, 2014. Applicants must present a graduation certificate for completion of an ATP certification training program with any ATP (ATM test code) knowledge test results dated after July 31, 2014.*

3. meet the minimum aeronautical experience requirements and provide the appropriate documentation prescribed in 14 CFR part 61, section 61.160

4. have a minimum of a third-class medical certificate, if a medical certificate is required (if any portion of the certification must occur in an actual airplane, then a medical certificate is required for that portion)

5. be at least 21 years of age

6. be able to read, speak, write, and understand the English language. If there is any doubt, consult AC 60-28, English Language Skill Standards Required by 14 CFR parts 61, 63, and 65, or contact your local Flight Standards District Office (FSDO). The examiner must determine whether the applicant meets the English language requirements before beginning the practical test

## Practical Test Prerequisites: Airline Transport Pilot Single-Engine Class

An applicant for the original issuance of an airplane category Airline Transport Pilot Single-Engine class certificate after July 31, 2014, is required (prior to taking the practical test) by 14 CFR part 61 to:

1. have passed an ATP aeronautical knowledge airplane airline transport pilot knowledge test (test code ATS, ATP, ATA, or ARA) within 24 months before the date of the practical test except for employees of (or employed by):

   a. flight crewmembers employed by part 119 certificate holders and that have passed the operator's approved pilot-in-command training or checking program,

   b. by the U.S. Armed Forces as a flight crew member at the time of the practical test in U.S. military air transport operations and has completed the pilot-in-command aircraft qualification training program appropriate to the pilot certificate and rating sought.

NOTE: *Applicants qualified by a and b qualify for the practical test with an expired ATP knowledge test.*

2. have the aeronautical experience prescribed in 14 CFR part 61, that applies to the airplane single-engine category and class rating

3. have a minimum of a third-class medical certificate, if a medical certificate is required (if any portion of the certification must occur in an actual airplane, then a medical certificate is required for that portion)

4. be at least 23 years of age

5. be able to read, speak, write, and understand the English language. If there is any doubt, consult AC 60-28, English Language Skill Standards Required by 14 CFR parts 61, 63, and 65, or contact your local Flight Standards District Office (FSDO). The examiner must determine whether the applicant meets the English language requirements before beginning the practical test

In accordance with the requirements of 14 CFR part 61, section 61.153(b) and ICAO aviation English Language proficiency requirements, the entire application process and testing procedures must be accomplished fluently enough in the English language such that crew coordination and communication is never in doubt.

## *Practical Test Prerequisites: Aircraft Type Rating*

An applicant for a type rating in an airplane is required by 14 CFR part 61 to have:

1. the applicable experience
2. a minimum of a third-class medical certificate, if a medical certificate is required (not required for simulator)
3. the appropriate category and class rating, or accomplish the appropriate Tasks in the private/commercial pilot Practical Test Standards
4. received and logged ground training from an authorized ground or flight instructor and flight training from an authorized flight instructor, on the Areas of Operation in this practical test standard that apply to the aircraft type rating sought
5. received a logbook endorsement from the instructor who conducted the training, certifying that the applicant completed all the training on the Areas of Operation in this practical test standard that apply to the aircraft type rating sought

If the applicant is an employee of a part 121 or part 135 certificate holder, the applicant may present a training record that shows the satisfactory completion of that certificate holder's approved pilot in command training program for the aircraft type rating sought, instead of the requirements of 4 and 5 above.

An applicant who holds a private pilot or limited commercial pilot certificate is required to have passed the appropriate instrument rating knowledge test since the beginning of the 24th month before the practical test is taken if the test is for the concurrent issuance of an instrument rating and an aircraft type rating.

If an applicant is taking a practical test for the issuance of a private or commercial pilot certificate with an airplane rating, in an aircraft that requires a type rating, private pilot practical test standards or commercial pilot practical test standards, as appropriate to the certificate, must be used in conjunction with this PTS. Also, the current instrument rating practical test standard must be used in conjunction with this PTS if the applicant is concurrently taking a practical test for the issuance of an instrument rating and a type rating. The Tasks that are in the private pilot, commercial pilot, or instrument rating PTS (and not listed in this PTS) must be accomplished.

An amphibian type rating must bear the limitation "Limited to Land" or "Limited to Sea," as appropriate, unless the applicant demonstrates proficiency in both land and sea operations.

*FAA-S-8081-5F*

**Change 1 (12/16/2008) & Change 4 (4/4/2012)**

## *Aircraft Type Ratings Limited to "VFR Only"*

Pilot applicants who wish to add a type rating, limited to VFR, to their certificate must take a practical test that includes the following items:

### Section 1: Preflight Preparation

#### Area of Operation I: Preflight Preparation

   Task A:  Equipment Examination
   Task B:  Performance and Limitations

### Section 2: Preflight Procedures, Inflight Maneuvers, and Postflight Procedures

#### Area of Operation II: Preflight Procedures

   Task A:  Preflight Inspection
   Task B:  Powerplant Start
   Task C:  Taxiing
   Task F:  Pre-takeoff Checks

#### Area of Operation III: Takeoff and Departure Phase

   Task A:  Normal and Crosswind Takeoff
   Task F:  Powerplant Failure during Takeoff
   Task G:  Rejected Takeoff

#### Area of Operation IV: Inflight Maneuvers

   Task A:  Steep Turns
   Task B:  Approaches to Stalls
   Task C:  Powerplant Failure—Multiengine Airplane
   Task D:  Powerplant Failure—Single-engine Airplane
   Task E:  Specific Flight Characteristics

#### Area of Operation V: Instrument Procedures—Not Applicable

#### Area of Operation VI: Landings and Approaches to Landings

   Task A:  Normal and Crosswind Approaches and Landings
   Task B:  Approach and Landing with (Simulated) Powerplant Failure—Multiengine Airplane
   Task H:  Rejected Landing
   Task I:  Landing from a No Flap or a Nonstandard Flap Approach

### Area of Operation VII: Normal and Abnormal Procedures

Task A:   Normal and Abnormal Procedures

### Area of Operation VIII: Emergency Procedures

Task A:   Emergency Procedures

### Area of Operation IX: Postflight Procedures—All Tasks as Applicable

## Removal of the "Limited to Center Thrust" Limitation or Initial ATP/type rating Airplane Multiengine Class Certificate

Any ATP/type rating applicant must show evidence of a satisfactory completed evaluation of multiengine airplane class maneuvers by holding one of the following:

1.   FAA commercial (or ATP) certificate with multiengine and instrument rating at the commercial pilot certificate level not limited to center thrust.
2.   Military multiengine PIC instrument qualification meeting 14 CFR 61.73 requirements in an airplane having published $V_{MC}$ (ie. C-12, C-130, C-17, etc.).
3.   Current foreign ATP or current foreign commercial license with instrument privileges and multiengine privileges (without a PIC restriction for multiengine privileges).

*NOTE:*   *Foreign pilot applicants must have obtained a letter of authenticity from AFS-760 that indicates the applicant holds a foreign ATP or commercial license with either a current multiengine class rating or current type rating in a multiengine airplane.*

Applicants not meeting the above requirements must be tested and satisfactorily perform the following Areas of Operation and Tasks from FAA-S-8081-5 (as amended), *Airline Transport Pilot Practical Test Standards for Airplane*, and the following Areas of Operation and Tasks from FAA-S-8081-12 (as amended), *Commercial Pilot Practical Test Standards for Airplane*, during the practical test in a multiengine airplane that has a manufacturer's published $V_{MC}$ speed. FAA-S-8081-12 simulation device credit tables are not applicable. All tasks may be accomplished in qualified simulators.

From FAA-S-8081-5, *Airline Transport Pilot and Aircraft Type Rating Practical Test Standards—Airplane*:

### Area of Operation III: Takeoff and Departure Phase

Task F:   Powerplant Failure During Takeoff
Task G:   Rejected Takeoff

### Area of Operation IV: Inflight Maneuvers

Task C: Powerplant Failure—Multiengine Airplane

## Area of Operation VI: Landings and Approaches to Landings

Task C: Approach and Landing with (Simulated) Powerplant Failure—Multiengine Airplane

From FAA-S-8081-12, *Commercial Pilot Practical Test Standards—Airplane, Section II: Commercial Pilot Airplane—Multiengine Land and Multiengine Sea*:

## Area of Operation I: Preflight Preparation

Task H: Principles of Flight—Engine Inoperative

## Area of Operation X: Multiengine Operations

Task A: Maneuvering with One Engine Inoperative
Task B: $V_{MC}$ Demonstration

**NOTE:** *A flight simulator or flight training device representative of a multiengine airplane, with a manufacturer's published $V_{MC}$ speed, may be used if used in accordance with a program approved for a 14 CFR part 142 certificate holder.*

## Aircraft and Equipment Required for the Practical Test

If the practical test is conducted in an aircraft, the applicant is required by 14 CFR part 61 to provide an appropriate and airworthy aircraft for use during the practical test. Its operating limitations must not prohibit the Tasks required on the practical test. Multiengine certification flight checks require normal engine shutdowns and restarts in the air to include propeller feathering and unfeathering. The AFM must not prohibit these procedures. (Low power settings for cooling periods prior to the actual shutdown are acceptable and encouraged as the AFM states.) The exception is for type ratings when that particular airplane was not certificated with inflight unfeathering capability. For those airplanes ONLY, simulated powerplant failures will suffice.

Flight instruments are those required for controlling the aircraft without outside references. The required radio equipment is that which is necessary for communications with ATC, and for the performance of instrument approach procedures. GPS equipment must be instrument certified and contain the current database.

If the practical test is conducted in an aircraft, the applicant is required to provide an appropriate view limiting device that is acceptable to the examiner. The device must be used during all testing that requires testing "solely by reference to instruments." This device must prevent the applicant from having visual reference outside the aircraft, but not prevent the examiner from having visual reference outside the aircraft. A procedure should be established between the applicant and the examiner as to when and how this device should be donned and removed and this procedure briefed before the flight.

The applicant is expected to demonstrate automation management skills in utilizing the autopilot, avionics and systems displays, and/or flight management system (FMS), as applicable to installed equipment, during the practical test to assist in the management of the aircraft. The examiner is expected to test the applicant's knowledge of the systems that are installed and operative during the oral and flight portions of the practical test. This is specifically to include meanings and limitations of airport, taxiway, and runway signs, lights, and markings.

If the practical test is conducted in the aircraft and the aircraft has an operable and properly installed GPS, the applicant must demonstrate GPS approach proficiency. If the applicant has contracted for training in an approved course that includes GPS training, and the airplane/simulator/FTD has a properly installed and operable GPS, the applicant must demonstrate GPS approach proficiency. When a practical test is conducted for a 14 CFR part 121/135 operator, the operator's approved training program is controlling.

**NOTE:** *The applicant must perform the tasks, except for water operations, in actual or simulated instrument conditions unless the practical test cannot be accomplished under instrument flight rules because the aircraft's type certificate makes the aircraft incapable of operating under instrument flight rules.*

### Use of an FAA-Approved Flight Simulator or Flight Training Device

In the Area of Operations labeled "Preflight Preparation," the Tasks are knowledge only. These Tasks do not require the use of a flight training device (FTD), flight simulator, or an aircraft to accomplish, but they may be used.

Each inflight maneuver or procedure must be performed by the applicant in an FTD, flight simulator, or an aircraft. Appendix 1 of this practical test standard should be consulted to identify the maneuvers or procedures that may be accomplished in an FTD or flight simulator. The level of FTD or flight simulator required for each maneuver or procedure is also found in appendix 1.

When accomplished in an aircraft, certain Task elements may be accomplished through "simulated" actions in the interest of safety and practicality, but when accomplished in an FTD or flight simulator, these same actions would not be "simulated." For example, when in an aircraft, a simulated engine fire may be addressed by retarding the throttle to idle, simulating the shutdown of the engine, simulating the discharge of the fire suppression agent, and simulating the disconnection of associated electrics, hydraulics, pneumatics, etc.

However, when the same emergency condition is addressed in an FTD or a flight simulator, all Task elements must be accomplished as would be expected under actual circumstances. Similarly, safety of flight precautions taken in the aircraft for the accomplishment of a specific maneuver or procedure (such as limiting the altitude in an approach to stall, or setting maximum airspeed for a rejected takeoff) need not be taken when an FTD or a flight simulator is used.

It is important to understand that whether accomplished in an FTD, a flight simulator, or the aircraft, all Tasks and Task elements for each maneuver or procedure will have the same performance criteria applied for determination of overall satisfactory performance.

### Examiner Responsibility

The examiner who conducts the practical test is responsible for determining that the applicant meets the standards outlined in the Objective of each Task within the Areas of Operation in the practical test standard. The examiner must meet this responsibility by determining that the applicant's knowledge and skill meet the Objective in all required Tasks.

In accordance with the requirements of 14 CFR 61.153(b) and ICAO English Language proficiency requirements, the examiner must accomplish the entire application process and test in the English language. The English language component of crew coordination and communication skills can never be in doubt for the satisfactory outcome of the test. Normal restatement of questions as would be done for a native English speaking applicant is still permitted and **not** grounds for disqualification.

The equipment examination in Section 1 must be closely coordinated and related to the flight portion of the practical test in Section 2, but must not be given during the flight portion of the practical test. The equipment examination should be administered prior (it may be the same day) to the flight portion of the practical test. The examiner may accept written evidence of the equipment exam if the exam is approved by the Administrator and administered by an individual authorized by the Administrator. The examiner must use whatever means deemed suitable to determine that the applicant's equipment knowledge meets the standard.

The Areas of Operation in Section 2 contain Tasks, which include both "knowledge" and "skill" elements. The examiner must ask the applicant to perform the skill elements. Knowledge elements not evident in the demonstrated skills may be tested by questioning, at any time, during the flight event. This specifically should include meanings and limitations of airport, taxiway, and runway signs, lights, and markings. Questioning inflight should be used judiciously so that safety is not jeopardized. Questions may be deferred until after the flight portion of the test is completed.

For aircraft requiring only one pilot, the examiner may not assist the applicant in the management of the aircraft, radio communications, tuning and identifying navigational equipment, or using navigation charts. If the examiner, other than an FAA Inspector, is qualified and current in the specific make and model aircraft that is certified for two or more crewmembers, he or she may occupy a duty position.

If the examiner occupies a duty position on an aircraft that requires two or more crewmembers, the examiner must fulfill the duties of that position. Moreover, when occupying a required duty position, the examiner must perform crew resource management (CRM) functions as briefed and requested by the applicant except during the accomplishment of steep turns and approach to stalls. During these two Tasks the applicant must demonstrate their ability to control the aircraft without the intervention from the non-flying pilot.

Safety of Flight must be the prime consideration at all times. The examiner, applicant, and crew must be constantly alert for other traffic.

### Satisfactory Performance

The ability of an applicant to safely perform the required Tasks is based on:

1.  performing the Tasks specified in the Areas of Operation for the certificate or rating sought within the approved standards;
2.  demonstrating mastery of the aircraft with the successful outcome of each Task performed never seriously in doubt (14 CFR section 61.43(a)(2));

3.    demonstrating satisfactory proficiency and competency within the approved standards and single-pilot competence if the aircraft is type certificated for single-pilot operations; and

4.    demonstrating sound judgment and single-pilot resource management/crew resource management.

"Knowledge" means the applicant can describe in general or specific terms a response to the examiner's question.

"Satisfactory knowledge" means the applicant's answer contains at least 70 percent of the reference answer to the examiner's question ("textbook answer") and if the applicant's actions followed his/her response, the safety of the airplane would never be seriously in doubt.

## Unsatisfactory Performance

The tolerances represent the performance expected in good flying conditions. If, in the judgment of the examiner, the applicant does not meet the standards of performance of any Task performed, the associated Area of Operation is failed and therefore, the practical test is failed.

**NOTE:**    *The tolerances stated in this standard are intended to be used as a measurement of the applicant's ability to operate in the instrument environment. They provide guidance for examiners to use in judging the applicant's qualifications. The regulations governing the tolerances for operation under Instrument Flight Rules are established in 14 CFR part 91.*

The examiner or applicant may discontinue the test at any time when the failure of an Area of Operation makes the applicant ineligible for the certificate or rating sought. **The test may be continued ONLY with the consent of the applicant.** If the test is discontinued, the applicant is entitled credit for only those Areas of Operation and their associated Tasks satisfactorily performed. However, during the retest, and at the discretion of the examiner, any Task may be reevaluated, including those previously passed.

Typical areas of unsatisfactory performance and grounds for disqualification are:

1.    Any action or lack of action by the applicant that requires corrective intervention by the examiner to maintain safe flight.

2.    Failure to use proper and effective visual scanning techniques, when applicable, to clear the area before and while performing maneuvers.

3.    Consistently exceeding tolerances stated in the Objectives.

4.   Failure to take prompt corrective action when tolerances are exceeded.

When a Notice of Disapproval is issued, the examiner shall record the applicant's unsatisfactory performance in terms of the Area of Operation and specific Task(s) not meeting the standard appropriate to the practical test conducted. The Area(s) of Operation/Task(s) not tested and the number of practical test failures shall also be recorded. If the applicant fails the practical test because of a special emphasis area, the Notice of Disapproval shall indicate the associated Task. For example, Area of Operation VI, Task D, Landing From a Circling Approach, failure to avoid runway incursion.

### *Letter of Discontinuance*

When a practical test is discontinued for reasons other than unsatisfactory performance (i.e., equipment failure, weather, illness), The FAA Form 8710-1, Airman Certificate and/or Rating Application, and, if applicable, the Airman Knowledge Test Report, is returned to the applicant. The examiner then must prepare, sign, and issue a Letter of Discontinuance to the applicant. The Letter of Discontinuance must identify the Areas of Operation and their associated Tasks of the practical test that were successfully completed. The applicant must be advised that the Letter of Discontinuance must be presented to the examiner, to receive credit for the items successfully completed, when the practical test is resumed, and made part of the certification file.

### *Aeronautical Decision Making (ADM) and Risk Management*

The examiner must evaluate the applicant's ability throughout the practical test to use good aeronautical decision making procedures in order to evaluate risks. The examiner must accomplish this requirement by developing scenarios that incorporate as many Tasks as possible to evaluate the applicant's risk management in making safe aeronautical decisions. For example, the examiner may develop a scenario that incorporates weather decisions and performance planning. Information may be found in AC 60-22, Aeronautical Decision Making, and many other resources as well.

### *Crew Resource Management (CRM and Single Pilot Resource Management (SRM))*

CRM/SRM "…refers to the effective use of all available resources: human resources, hardware, and information. Other groups routinely working with the cockpit crew (or single pilot) who are involved in decisions required to operate a flight safely are also essential participants in an effective CRM process. These groups include, but are not limited to: dispatchers, flight attendants, maintenance personnel, flight operations managers, management, pilot examiners, check airmen, flight standards officers, and air traffic controllers." CRM/SRM is not a single Task. CRM/SRM is a set of competencies, which must be evident in all Tasks in this practical test standard, as applied to the single-pilot or the multicrew operation. CRM focuses on situational awareness, communication skills, teamwork, task allocation, and decision making within a comprehensive framework of standard operating procedures (SOP). SRM is the management of all resources onboard the aircraft and available from outside resources to the single pilot.

CRM/SRM deficiencies almost always contribute to the unsatisfactory performance of a Task. For debriefing purposes, an amplified list of CRM competencies, expressed as behavioral markers, may be found in AC 120-51, as amended, Crew Resource Management Training. These markers consider the use of various levels of automation in flight management systems.

CRM/SRM evaluations are still largely subjective. Certain CRM competencies are well-suited to objective evaluation. These are the CRM-related practices set forth in the aircraft manufacturer's or the operator's FAA-approved operating or training manuals as explicit, required procedures. The CRM procedures may be associated with one or more Tasks in these practical test standards. Examples include required briefings, radio calls, and instrument approach callouts. The evaluator simply observes that the individual complies (or fails to comply) with requirements.

### How the Examiner Evaluates CRM/SRM

Examiners are required to exercise proper CRM/SRM competencies in conducting tests, as well as expecting the same from applicants.

Pass/Fail judgments based solely on CRM/SRM issues must be carefully chosen since they may be entirely subjective. Those Pass/Fail judgments, which are not subjective, apply to CRM-related procedures in FAA-approved operations manuals that must be accomplished, such as briefings to other crewmembers. In such cases, the operator (or the aircraft manufacturer) specifies what should be briefed and when the briefings should occur.

The examiner may judge objectively whether the briefings should occur. The examiner may judge objectively whether the briefing requirement was or was not met. In those cases where the operator (or aircraft manufacturer) has not specified a briefing, the examiner shall require the applicant to brief the appropriate items from the following note. The examiner may then judge objectively whether the briefing requirement was or was not met.

**NOTE:** *The majority of aviation accidents and incidents are due to resource management failures by the pilot/crew; fewer are due to technical failures. Each applicant must give a crew briefing before each takeoff/departure and approach/landing. If the operator or aircraft manufacturer* *has not specified a briefing, the briefing must cover the appropriate items, such as: departure runway, DP/STAR/IAP, power settings, speeds, abnormal or emergency procedures prior to or after reaching decision speed (i.e., $V_1$ or $V_{MC}$), emergency return intentions, missed approach procedures, FAF, altitude at FAF, initial rate of descent, DA/DH/MDA, time to missed approach, and what is expected of the other crewmembers during the takeoff/DP and approach/landing. If the first takeoff/departure and approach/landing briefings are satisfactory, the examiner may allow the applicant to brief only the changes, during the remainder of the flight.*

## Applicant's Use of Checklists

Throughout the practical test, the applicant is evaluated on the use of an appropriate checklist. In crew served airplanes, the applicant as PIC (acting) should coordinate all checklists with the crew to ensure all items are accomplished in a timely manner. The applicant as acting PIC should manage the flight to include crew checklist performance, requiring standard callouts, announcing intentions, and initiating checklist procedures. If the airplane is a single-pilot airplane, the applicant should demonstrate CRM principles described as single pilot resource management (SRM). Proper use is dependent on the specific Task being evaluated. The situation may be such that the use of the checklist, while accomplishing elements of an Objective, would be either unsafe or impractical, especially in a single-pilot operation. In this case, a review of the checklist after the elements have been accomplished would be appropriate. Use of a checklist should also consider visual scanning and division of attention at all times.

## Use of Distractions during Practical Tests

Numerous studies indicate that many accidents have occurred when the pilot has been distracted during critical phases of flight. To evaluate the pilot's ability and situational awareness to utilize proper control technique while dividing attention both inside and outside the cockpit, the examiner must cause a realistic distraction during the flight portion of the practical test to evaluate the applicant's ability to divide attention while maintaining safe flight.

## Positive Exchange of Flight Controls

During the flight, there must always be a clear understanding between the pilots of who has control of the aircraft. Prior to flight, a briefing should be conducted that includes the procedure for the exchange of flight controls. Some operators have established a two-step procedure for exchange of flight controls. A popular three-step process in the exchange of flight controls between the pilots is explained below. Any safe procedure agreed to by the applicant and the examiner is acceptable.

When one pilot wishes to give the other pilot control of the aircraft, he or she will say, "you have the flight controls." The other pilot acknowledges immediately by saying, "I have the flight controls." The first pilot again says, "you have the flight controls." When control is returned to the first pilot, follow the same procedure. A visual check is recommended to verify that the exchange has occurred. There should never be any doubt as to who is flying the aircraft.

# Section 1:

# Preflight Preparation

*(this page intentionally left blank)*

# Areas of Operation

## I.    Preflight Preparation

### Task A:    Equipment Examination

*References:*    *AC 20-29, AC 20-117, AC 91-43, AC 91-51,*
*AC 91-74, AC 120-60, AC 135-17, 14 CFR part 61;*
*POH; AFM.*

**Objective:**    To determine that the applicant:

1.    Exhibits satisfactory knowledge appropriate to the airplane;
its systems and components; its normal, abnormal, and
emergency procedures; and uses the correct terminology
with regard to the following items—

a.    landing gear—extension/retraction system(s);
indicators, float devices, brakes, antiskid, tires, nose-
wheel steering, and shock absorbers.

b.    powerplant—controls and indications, induction
system, carburetor and fuel injection, turbocharging,
cooling, fire detection/protection, mounting points,
turbine wheels, compressors, deicing, anti-icing, and
other related components.

c.    propellers—type, controls, feathering/unfeathering,
auto-feather, negative torque sensing, synchronizing,
and synchrophasing.

d.    fuel system—capacity; drains; pumps; controls;
indicators; cross-feeding; transferring; jettison; fuel
grade, color and additives; fueling and defueling
procedures; and fuel substitutions, if applicable.

e.    oil system—capacity, grade, quantities, and indicators.

f.    hydraulic system—capacity, pumps, pressure,
reservoirs, grade, and regulators.

g.    electrical system—alternators, generators, battery,
circuit breakers and protection devices, controls,
indicators, and external and auxiliary power sources
and ratings.

h.    environmental systems—heating, cooling, ventilation,
oxygen and pressurization, controls, indicators, and
regulating devices.

i.    avionics and communications—autopilot; flight director;
Electronic Flight Instrument Systems (EFIS); Flight
Management System(s) (FMS); Doppler Radar; Inertial
Navigation Systems (INS); Global Positioning System/
Wide Area Augmentation System/Local Area
Augmentation System (GPS/WAAS/LAAS); VOR,
NDB, ILS, GLS, RNAV systems and components;

traffic (MLS deleted) awareness/warning/avoidance systems, terrain awareness/warning/alert systems; other avionics or communications equipment, as appropriate; indicating devices; transponder; and emergency locator transmitter.

j.   ice protection—anti-ice, deice, pitot-static system protection, propeller, windshield, wing and tail surfaces.

k.   crewmember and passenger equipment—oxygen system, survival gear, emergency exits, evacuation procedures and crew duties, and quick donning oxygen mask for crewmembers and passengers.

l.   flight controls—ailerons, elevator(s), rudder(s), control tabs, balance tabs, stabilizer, flaps, spoilers, leading edge flaps/slats and trim systems.

m.   pitot-static system with associated instruments and the power source for the flight instruments.

2.   Exhibits satisfactory knowledge of the contents of the POH or AFM with regard to the systems and components listed in paragraph 1 (above); the Minimum Equipment List (MEL) and/or configuration deviation list (CDL), if appropriate; and the operations specifications, if applicable.

## Task B:  *Performance and Limitations*

*References*   *14 CFR parts 1, 61, 91; AFD; POH; AFM; AIM; AC 20-117, AC 91-51, AC 91-74, AC 91-79, AC 120-27; AC 120-60, AC 135-17 FAA-H-8083-1, FAA-H-8083-3, FAA-H-8083-23, FAA-H-8083-25.*

**Objective:**   To determine that the applicant:

1.   Exhibits satisfactory knowledge of performance and limitations, including a thorough knowledge of the adverse effects of exceeding any limitation.

2.   Demonstrates proficient use of (as appropriate to the airplane) performance charts, tables, graphs, or other data relating to items, such as—

a. Departure airport, taxiway, and runway NOTAMs, runway usable lengths, HOT Spots, taxi restrictions, specific taxi procedures, as applicable, and signage/markings

b. accelerate-stop distance.

c. accelerate-go distance.

d. takeoff performance—all engines and with engine(s) inoperative.

e. climb performance including segmented climb performance with all engines operating—with one or more engine(s) inoperative, and with other engine malfunctions as may be appropriate.

f. service ceiling—all engines, with engines(s) inoperative, including drift down, if appropriate.

g. cruise performance.

h. fuel consumption, range, and endurance.

i. descent performance.

j. Arrival airport, taxiway, and runway NOTAMs, runway usable lengths, HOT Spots, tax restrictions, specific tax procedures as applicable, and signage/markings.

k. landing distance.

l. land and hold short operations (LAHSO).

m. go-around from rejected landings (landing climb).

n. other performance data (appropriate to the airplane).

3. Describes (as appropriate to the airplane) the airspeeds used during specific phases of flight.

4. Describes the effects of meteorological conditions upon performance characteristics and correctly applies these factors to a specific chart, table, graph, or other performance data.

5. Computes the center-of-gravity location for a specific load condition (as specified by the examiner), including adding, removing, or shifting weight.

6. Determines if the computed center-of-gravity is within the forward and aft center-of-gravity limits, and that lateral fuel balance is within limits for takeoff and landing.

7. Demonstrates adequate knowledge of the adverse effects of airframe icing during pre-takeoff, takeoff, cruise and landing phases of flight and corrective actions.

8.  Demonstrates adequate knowledge of procedures for wing contamination recognition and adverse effects of airframe icing during pre-takeoff, takeoff, cruise, and landing phases of flight. (Pilots applying for an aircraft type rating should have adequate knowledge of icing procedures and/or available information published by the manufacturer that is specific to that type of aircraft.)

9.  Demonstrates good planning and knowledge of procedures in applying operational factors affecting airplane performance.

10. Demonstrates knowledge of the stabilized approach procedures and the decision criteria for go-around or rejected landings.

### Task C: Water and Seaplane Characteristics (AMES/ASES)

*References: 14 CFR part 61; FAA-H-8083-3, FAA-H-8083-23.*

**Objective:** To determine that the applicant exhibits knowledge of the elements related to water and seaplane characteristics by explaining:

1.  The characteristics of a water surface as affected by features, such as—

    a.  size and location
    b.  direction and strength of the water current
    c.  presence of floating and partially submerged debris.
    d.  protected and unprotected areas
    e.  effect of surface wind and method of determining its force
    f.  operating near sandbars, islands, and shoals
    g.  other pertinent characteristics deemed important by the examiner

2.  Float and hull construction and their effect on seaplane/flying boat performance.

3.  Causes of porpoising and skipping, and pilot action to prevent or correct these occurrences.

### Task D: Seaplane Bases, Maritime Rules, and Aids to Marine Navigation (AMES/ASES)

*References: AIM; FAA-H-8083-3, FAA-H-8083-23.*

**Objective:** To determine that the applicant exhibits satisfactory knowledge of the elements related to seaplane bases, maritime rules, and aids to marine navigation by explaining:

1. How to identify and locate seaplane bases on charts or in directories.
2. Operating restrictions at seaplane bases.
3. Right-of-way, steering, and sailing rules pertinent to seaplane operation.
4. Purpose and identification of marine navigation aids, such as buoys, beacons, lights, and range markers.
5. Naval Vessel Protection Zones.
6. No Wake Zones.

*(this page intentionally left blank)*

# Section 2:

# Preflight Procedures, Inflight Maneuvers, and

# Postflight Procedures

*FAA-S-8081-5F*

*(this page intentionally left blank)*

# Areas of Operation

## II. Preflight Procedures

### Task A: Preflight Inspection

References: 14 CFR parts 61, 91; POH/AFM; AC 20-29,
AC 20-117, AC 61-84, AC 91-43, AC-51, AC 91-74,
AC 120-27, AC 120-60, AC 135-17.

NOTE: If a flight engineer (FE) is a required crewmember for a
particular type airplane, the actual visual inspection may be
waived. The actual visual inspection may be replaced by
using an approved pictorial means that realistically portrays
the location and detail of inspection items. On airplanes
requiring an FE, an applicant must demonstrate satisfactory
knowledge of the FE functions for the safe completion of
the flight if the FE becomes ill or incapacitated during a
flight.

Objective: To determine that the applicant:

1. Exhibits satisfactory knowledge of the preflight inspection
   procedures, while explaining briefly—

   a. the purpose of inspecting the items which must be
      checked.
   b. how to detect possible defects.
   c. the corrective action to take.

2. Exhibits satisfactory knowledge of the operational status of
   the airplane by locating and explaining the significance and
   importance of related documents, such as—

   a. airworthiness and registration certificates.
   b. operating limitations, handbooks, and manuals.
   c. minimum equipment list (MEL), if appropriate.
   d. weight and balance data.
   e. maintenance requirements, tests, and appropriate
      records applicable to the proposed flight or operation;
      and maintenance that may be performed by the pilot or
      other designated crewmember.

3. Uses the appropriate checklist or coordinates with crew to
   ensure completion of checklist items in a timely manner and
   as recommended by the manufacturer or approved method
   to inspect the airplane externally and internally.

4. Verifies the airplane is safe for flight by emphasizing (as
   appropriate) the need to look at and explain the purpose of
   inspecting items, such as—

a. powerplant, including controls and indicators.
b. fuel quantity, grade, type, contamination safeguards, and servicing procedures.
c. oil quantity, grade, and type.
d. hydraulic fluid quantity, grade, type, and servicing procedures.
e. oxygen quantity, pressures, servicing procedures, and associated systems and equipment for crew and passengers.
f. hull, landing gear, float devices, brakes, steering system, winglets, and canards.
g. tires for condition, inflation, and correct mounting, where applicable.
h. fire protection/detection systems for proper operation, servicing, pressures, and discharge indications.
i. pneumatic system pressures and servicing.
j. ground environmental systems for proper servicing and operation.
k. auxiliary power unit (APU) for servicing and operation.
l. flight control systems including trim, spoilers, and leading/trailing edge.
m. anti-ice, deice systems, servicing, and operation.
n. installed and auxiliary aircraft security equipment, as appropriate.

5. Coordinates with ground crew and ensures adequate clearance prior to moving any devices, such as door, hatches, and flight control surfaces.
6. Complies with the provisions of the appropriate operations specifications, if applicable, as they pertain to the particular airplane and operation.
7. Demonstrates proper operation of all applicable airplane systems.
8. Notes any discrepancies, determines if the airplane is airworthy and safe for flight, or takes the proper corrective action, and acknowledges limitations imposed by MEL/CDL items.
9. Checks the general area around the airplane for hazards to the safety of the airplane and personnel.
10. Ensures that the airplane and surfaces are free of ice, snow, and has satisfactory knowledge of deicing procedures, if icing conditions were present or ice was found.

## Task B:   Powerplant Start

*References:   14 CFR part 61; POH/AFM.*

**Objective:**   To determine that the applicant:

1.   Exhibits adequate knowledge of the correct powerplant start procedures including the use of an auxiliary power unit (APU) or external power source, starting under various atmospheric conditions, normal and abnormal starting limitations, and the proper action required in the event of a malfunction.
2.   Ensures the ground safety procedures are followed during the before-start, start, and after-start phases.
3.   Ensures the use of appropriate ground crew personnel during the start procedures.
4.   Performs all items of the start procedures by systematically following the approved checklist procedure in a timely manner and as recommended by the manufacturer for the before-start, start, and after-start phases.
5.   Demonstrates sound judgment and operating practices in those instances where specific instructions or checklist items are not published.

## Task C:   TAXIING

*References:   14 CFR part 61; POH/AFM; AC 91-73, AC 120-57, AC 120-74.*

**Objective:**   To determine that the applicant:

1.   Exhibits adequate knowledge of safe taxi procedures (as appropriate to the airplane including push-back or power-back, as may be applicable).
2.   Demonstrating and explaining procedures for holding the pilot's workload to a minimum during taxi operations .
3.   Exhibiting taxi operation planning procedures, such as recording taxi instructions, reading back taxi clearances, and reviewing taxi routes on the airport diagram.
4.   Demonstrating procedures to insure that clearance or instructions that are actually received are adhered to rather than the ones expected to be received.
5.   Know, explain and discuss the hazards of low visibility operations.

6. Demonstrates proficiency by maintaining correct and positive airplane control. In airplanes equipped with float devices, this includes water taxiing, sailing, step taxiing, approaching a buoy, and docking.
7. Maintains proper spacing on other aircraft, obstructions, and persons.
8. Accomplishes the applicable checklist items or ensures all required checks as required by the appropriate checklist items are accomplished in a timely manner and as recommended by the manufacturer, and performs recommended procedures.
9. Maintains desired track and speed.
10. Complies with instructions issued by ATC (or the examiner simulating ATC).
11. Observes runway hold lines, localizer and glide slope critical areas, buoys, beacons, and other surface control and lighting.
12. Maintains constant vigilance and airplane control during taxi operation to prevent runway/waterway incursion.
13. Demonstrating and/or explaining procedural differences for night operations.
14. Demonstrating and explaining the use(s) of aircraft exterior lighting and differences for day and night operations.

## Task D:   Sailing (AMES/ASES)

*References:  POH/AFM; AIM; FAA-H-8083-3, FAA-H-8083-23.*

**Objective:**   To determine that the applicant:

1. Exhibits knowledge of the elements related to sailing by explaining the techniques used in this procedure.
2. Recognizes the circumstance when sailing should be used.
3. Plans and follows the most favorable course considering wind, water current, obstructions, debris, and other vessels.
4. Uses flight controls, flaps, doors, and water rudders, as appropriate, to follow the desired course.

## Task E:   Seaplane Base/Water Landing Site Markings and Lighting (AMES, ASES)

*References:  AIM; FAA-H-8083-3, FAA-H-8083-23.*

**Objective:**   To determine that the applicant:

1. Exhibits knowledge of the elements related to seaplane base/water landing site markings and lighting.
2. Identifies and interprets seaplane base/water landing site markings and lighting.

## Task F:    Pre-Takeoff Checks

*References:*   *14 CFR part 61; POH/AFM; AC 91-74, AC 120-60, AC 120-117.*

**Objective:**   To determine that the applicant:

1.   Exhibits satisfactory knowledge of the pre-takeoff checks by stating the reason for checking the items outlined on the approved checklist and explaining how to detect possible malfunctions.

2.   Divides attention properly inside and outside cockpit.

3.   Ensures that all systems are within their normal operating range prior to beginning, during the performance of, and at the completion of those checks required by the approved checklist.

4.   Explains, as may be requested by the examiner, any normal   or abnormal system-operating characteristic or limitation; and the corrective action for a specific malfunction.

5.   Determines if the airplane is safe for the proposed flight or requires maintenance.

6.   Determines the airplane's takeoff performance, considering such factors as wind, density altitude, weight, temperature, pressure altitude, and runway/waterway condition and length.

7.   Determines airspeeds/V-speeds and properly sets all instrument references, configures flight director and autopilot controls, and navigation and communications equipment to properly fly the aircraft in accordance with the ATC clearance.

8.   Reviews procedures for emergency and abnormal situations, which may be encountered during takeoff, and states the corrective action required of the pilot in command and other concerned crewmembers.

9.   Obtains and correctly interprets the takeoff and departure clearance as issued by ATC.

# III. Takeoff and Departure Phase

## Task A: Normal and Crosswind Takeoff

*References:* 14 CFR part 61; POH/AFM; FAA-H-8083-3;
AC 20-117, AC 91-54, AC 91-74.

**NOTE:** *VMC maneuver.*

**Objective:** To determine that the applicant:

1. Exhibits knowledge of normal and crosswind takeoffs and climbs including (as appropriate to the airplane) airspeeds, configurations, and emergency/abnormal procedures.
2. Notes any surface conditions, obstructions, aircraft cleared for LAHSO, or other hazards that might hinder a safe takeoff.
3. Verifies and correctly applies correction for the existing wind component to the takeoff performance.
4. Coordinates with crew (if crew served airplane) to ensure completion or completes required checks prior to starting takeoff to verify the expected powerplant performance. Performs or ensures all required pre-takeoff checks as required by the appropriate checklist items are accomplished in a timely manner and as recommended by the manufacturer.
5. Aligns the airplane on the runway centerline or clear of obstacles and vessels on waterways as appropriate.
6. Applies the controls correctly to maintain longitudinal alignment on the centerline of the runway, if appropriate, prior to initiating and during the takeoff.
7. Adjusts the powerplant controls as recommended by the FAA-approved guidance for the existing conditions.
8. Monitors powerplant controls, settings, and instruments during takeoff to ensure all predetermined parameters are maintained.
9. Adjusts the controls to attain the desired pitch attitude at the predetermined airspeed/V-speed to attain the desired performance for the particular takeoff segment.
10. Performs the required pitch changes and, as appropriate, performs or calls for and verifies the accomplishment of, gear and flap retractions, power adjustments, and other required pilot-related activities at the required airspeed/V-speeds within the tolerances established in the POH or AFM.
11. Uses the applicable noise abatement and wake turbulence avoidance procedures, as required.
12. Accomplishes, or calls for and verifies the accomplishment of, the appropriate checklist items in a timely manner and as recommended by the manufacturer.

13. Maintains the appropriate climb segment airspeed/V-speeds.
14. Maintains the desired heading, ±5°, and the desired airspeed (V-speed), ±5 knots (of the appropriate V-speed range).

## Task B: Glassy Water Takeoff and Climb (AMES/ASES)

*References: POH/AFM; FAA-H-8083-3, FAA-H-8083-23.*

**NOTE** *If a glassy water condition does not exist, the applicant's satisfactory knowledge of glassy water elements must be evaluated through oral testing. The applicant's skill must be evaluated by simulating the Task.*

**Objective:** To determine that the applicant:

1. Exhibits knowledge of the elements related to a glassy water takeoff and climb.
2. Positions the flight controls and flaps for the existing conditions.
3. Clears the area, notes any surface hazards and/or vessels prior to selecting a takeoff path.
4. Retracts the water rudders, if applicable.
5. Advances the throttles to takeoff power.
6. Avoids excessive water spray on the propellers.
7. Establishes and maintains an appropriate planing attitude, directional control, and corrects for porpoising, skipping, and increases in water drag.
8. Utilizes appropriate techniques to lift seaplane from the water surface.
9. Establishes proper attitude/airspeed, lifts off and accelerates to best single-engine climb speed or $V_Y$, whichever is greater, ±5 knots during the climb.
10. Reduces the flaps after a positive rate of climb is established and at a safe altitude.
11. Maintains takeoff power to a safe maneuvering altitude, then sets climb power.
12. Maintains directional control and proper wind-drift correction throughout takeoff and climb.
13. Uses noise abatement procedures, as required.
14. Completes appropriate checklists or ensures all required checks as required by the appropriate checklist items are accomplished in a timely manner and as recommended by the manufacturer.

## Task C: Rough Water Takeoff and Climb (AMES/ASES)

*References: POH/AFM; FAA-H-8083-3, FAA-H-8083-23.*

**NOTE:** *If a rough water condition does not exist, the applicant's satisfactory knowledge of rough water elements must be evaluated through oral testing. The applicant's skill must be evaluated by simulating the Task.*

**Objective:**   To determine that the applicant:

1.   Exhibits knowledge of the elements related to rough water takeoff and climb.
2.   Positions the flight controls and flaps for the existing conditions.
3.   Clears the area, selects the proper takeoff path, considering wind, swells, surface hazards and/or vessels.
4.   Retracts the water rudders, if applicable.
5.   Advances the throttles to takeoff power.
6.   Avoids excessive water spray on the propellers.
7.   Establishes and maintains an appropriate planing/lift-off attitude, directional control, and corrects for porpoising, skipping, or excessive bouncing.
8.   Establishes and maintains proper attitude to lift-off at minimum airspeed and accelerates to best single-engine climb speed or $V_Y$, whichever is greater, ±5 knots before leaving ground effect.
9.   Retracts the flaps after a positive rate of climb is established and at a safe altitude.
10.   Maintains takeoff power to a safe maneuvering altitude, then sets climb power.
11.   Maintains directional control and proper wind-drift correction throughout takeoff and climb.
12.   Uses noise abatement procedures, as required.
13.   Completes appropriate checklists or coordinates with crew to ensure completion of checklist items in a timely manner and as recommended by the manufacturer.

## Task D:   Confined-Area Takeoff and Climb (AMES/ASES)

*References:   POH/AFM; FAA-H-8083-3, FAA-H-8083-23.*

**NOTE:** *This Task simulates a takeoff from a small pond, which would require a takeoff and spiral climb; or a straight-ahead takeoff and climb from a narrow waterway with obstructions at either end. The examiner must evaluate both takeoff situations for this Task. In multiengine seaplanes with $V_X$ values within 5 knots of $V_{MC}$, the use of $V_Y$ or the manufacturer's recommendation may be more appropriate for this demonstration.*

**Objective:**   To determine that the applicant:

1.   Exhibits knowledge of the elements related to a confined-area takeoff and climb.

2. Positions the flight controls and flaps for the existing conditions.
3. Clears the area, notes any surface hazards, vessels, and/or obstructions prior to selecting a takeoff path.
4. Selects a takeoff path that will allow maximum safe utilization of wind, water, and low terrain.
5. Advances the throttles to takeoff power.
6. Ensures that the water rudders are retracted when no longer needed.
7. Maintains the most efficient alignment and planing angle, without skidding, porpoising, and skipping.
8. Lifts off at recommended airspeed and accelerates to manufacturer's recommended climb airspeed.
9. Climbs at manufacturer's recommended configuration and airspeed, or in their absence at $V_x$, +5/-0 knots until the obstacle is cleared.
10. After clearing all obstacles, accelerates to and maintains $V_y$, ±5 knots, retracts flaps and maintains safe bank angles while turning and/or providing best terrain clearance.
11. Maintains takeoff power to a safe altitude, and then sets climb power.
12. Uses noise abatement procedures, as required.
13. Completes appropriate checklists or coordinates with crew to ensure completion of checklist items in a timely manner and as recommended by the manufacturer.

## Task E: Instrument Takeoff

*References: 14 CFR part 61; POH/AFM; AIM; FAA-H-8083-15, FAA-H-8261-1; AC 20-117, AC 91-74, AC 135-17.*

**Objective:** To determine that the applicant:

1. Exhibits knowledge of an instrument takeoff with instrument meteorological conditions (IMC) simulated at or before reaching an altitude of 100 feet AGL. If accomplished in a flight simulator, visibility should be no greater than one-quarter (1/4) mile, or as specified by operator specifications, whichever is lower.
2. Takes into account, prior to beginning the takeoff, operational factors which could affect the maneuver, such as Takeoff Warning Inhibit Systems or other airplane characteristics, runway length, surface conditions, wind, wake turbulence, icing conditions, obstructions, and other related factors that could adversely affect safety.
3. Coordinates with crew, if a crew served airplane, or completes the appropriate checklist items in a timely manner and as recommended by the manufacturer in a

single pilot airplane, to ensure that the airplane systems applicable to the instrument takeoff are operating properly.

4. Sets the applicable avionics and flight instruments to the desired setting prior to initiating the takeoff.

5. Applies the controls correctly to maintain longitudinal alignment on the centerline of the runway, if appropriate, prior to initiating and during the takeoff.

6. Transitions smoothly and accurately from visual meteorological conditions (VMC) to actual or simulated instrument meteorological conditions (IMC).

7. Maintains the appropriate climb attitude.

8. Complies with the appropriate airspeeds/V-speeds and climb segment airspeeds.

9. Maintains desired heading within ±5° and desired airspeeds within ±5 knots.

10. Complies with ATC clearances and instructions issued by ATC (or the examiner simulating ATC).

11. Acknowledges and makes appropriate callouts to coordinate with the crew, if in a crew served airplane.

## Task F: Powerplant Failure during Takeoff

**NOTE:** *In a multiengine airplane certificated under 14 CFR parts 23 Commuter category, SFAR 41C 4(b), and part 25, with published $V_1$, $V_R$, and/or $V_2$ speeds, the failure of the most critical powerplant should be simulated at a point:*

1. *after $V_1$ and prior to $V_2$, if in the opinion of the examiner, it is appropriate under the prevailing conditions; or*

2. *as close as possible after $V_1$ when $V_1$ and $V_2$ or $V_1$ and $V_R$ are identical.*

*In a multiengine airplane certificated under 14 CFR part 23 (except commuter category), (for which no $V_1$, $V_R$, or $V_2$ speeds are published) the failure of the most critical powerplant should be simulated at a point after reaching a minimum of $V_{SSE}$ and, if accomplished in the aircraft, at an altitude not lower than 400 feet AGL, giving consideration to local atmospheric conditions, terrain, and aircraft performance available.*

*In a simulator, there are no limitations on powerplant failures in either airplane by certification basis.*

**APPLICANT NOTE:** *Expect this task to be combined with normal Task A, and/or Task E at examiner's discretion.*

*References: 14 CFR part 61; POH/AFM; FAA-H-8083-3, FSB Report.*

**Objective:** To determine that the applicant:

1. Exhibits satisfactory knowledge of the procedures used during powerplant failure on takeoff, the appropriate reference airspeeds, and the specific pilot actions required.
2. Takes into account, prior to beginning the takeoff, operational factors which could affect the maneuver, such as Takeoff Warning Inhibit Systems or other airplane characteristics, runway length, surface conditions, wind, wake turbulence, visibility, precipitation, obstructions, and other related factors that could adversely affect safety.
3. Completes required checks prior to starting takeoff to verify the expected powerplant performance. Performs all required pre-takeoff checks as required by the appropriate checklist items or coordinates with crew to ensure completion of checklist items in a timely manner and as recommended by the manufacturer.

4. Aligns the airplane on the runway/waterway.
5. Applies the controls correctly to maintain longitudinal alignment on the centerline of the runway, if appropriate, prior to initiating and during the takeoff.
6. Adjusts the powerplant controls as recommended by the FAA-approved guidance for the existing conditions.
7. Single-engine airplanes—establishes a power-off descent approximately straight-ahead, if the powerplant failure occurs after becoming airborne and before reaching an altitude where a safe turn can be made.
8. Continues the takeoff (in a 14 CFR part 25 or 14 CFR section 23.3(d) commuter multiengine airplane) if the (simulated) powerplant failure occurs at a point where the airplane can continue to a specified airspeed and altitude at the end of the runway commensurate with the airplane's performance capabilities and operating limitations.
9. Maintains (in a multiengine airplane), after a simulated powerplant failure and after a climb has been established, the desired heading within ±5°, desired airspeed within ±5 knots, and, if appropriate for the airplane, establishes a bank of approximately 5°, or as recommended by the manufacturer, toward the operating powerplant.
10. Maintains the airplane alignment with the heading appropriate for climb performance and terrain clearance when powerplant failure occurs.
11. Acknowledges and makes appropriate callouts to crew, if in crew served aircraft.

### Task G: Rejected Takeoff

References: 14 CFR part 61; FAA-H-8083-3; AC 120-62; POH/AFM.

**Objective:** To determine that the applicant understands when to reject or continue the takeoff and:

1. Exhibits satisfactory knowledge of the technique and procedure for accomplishing a rejected takeoff after powerplant/system(s) failure/warnings, including related safety factors.
2. Takes into account, prior to beginning the takeoff, operational actors, which could affect the maneuver, such as Takeoff Warning Inhibit Systems or other airplane characteristics, runway length, surface conditions, wind, visibility, precipitation, obstructions, and aircraft cleared for LAHSO that could affect takeoff performance and could adversely affect safety.
3. Aligns the airplane on the runway centerline or clear of obstacles and vessels on waterways.

4. Performs all required pre-takeoff checks as required by the appropriate checklist items or coordinates with crew to ensure completion of checklist items in a timely manner and as recommended by the manufacturer.

5. Adjusts the powerplant controls as recommended by the FAA-approved guidance for the existing conditions.

6. Applies the controls correctly to maintain longitudinal alignment on the centerline of the runway.

7. Aborts the takeoff if, in a single-engine airplane the powerplant failure occurs prior to becoming airborne, or in a multiengine airplane, the powerplant failure occurs at a point during the takeoff where the abort procedure can be initiated and the airplane can be safely stopped on the remaining runway/stopway. If a flight simulator is not used, the powerplant failure must be simulated before reaching 50 percent of $V_{MC}$.

8. Reduces the power smoothly and promptly, if appropriate to the airplane, when powerplant failure is recognized.

9. Uses spoilers, prop reverse, thrust reverse, wheel brakes, and other drag/braking devices, as appropriate, maintaining positive control in such a manner as to bring the airplane to a safe stop.

10. Accomplishes the appropriate powerplant failure or other procedures and/or checklists or coordinates with crew to ensure completion of checklist items in a timely manner and as recommended by the manufacturer, as set forth in the POH or AFM.

### Task H:    Departure Procedures

*References:   14 CFR part 61; AC 90-100; POH/AFM; AIM;  FAA-H-8261-1, FAA-H-8083-15.*

**Objective:**    To determine that the applicant:

1. In actual or simulated instrument conditions, exhibits satisfactory knowledge of DPs, En Route Low and High Altitude Charts, FMSP, and related pilot/controller responsibilities.

2. Uses the current and appropriate navigation publications for the proposed flight.

3. Selects, configures, and uses the appropriate communications frequencies, navigation and systems displays; selects and identifies the navigation aids and routes necessary to properly fly the assigned ATC clearance.

4. Coordinates with crew in crew served aircraft to ensure performance of, or performs the appropriate checklist items in a timely manner and as recommended by the manufacturer.

5. Establishes communications with ATC, using proper phraseology and advises ATC when unable to comply with a clearance or restriction.

6. Complies, in a timely manner, with all instructions and airspace restrictions.

7. Exhibits adequate knowledge of two-way radio communications failure procedures.

8. Intercepts, in a timely manner, all courses, radials, and bearings appropriate to the procedure, route, clearance, or as directed by the examiner.

9. Maintains the appropriate airspeed within ±10 knots, headings within ±10°, altitude within ±100 feet; and accurately tracks a course, radial, or bearing.

10. Conducts the departure phase to a point where, in the opinion of the examiner, the transition to the en route environment is complete.

# IV. Inflight Maneuvers

## Task A: Steep Turns

*References: 14 CFR part 61; FAA-H-8083-3; FSB Report; POH/AFM.*

**Objective:** To determine that the applicant:

1.  In actual or simulated instrument conditions, exhibits knowledge of steep turns (if applicable to the airplane) and the factors associated with performance; and, if applicable, wing loading, angle of bank, stall speed, pitch, power requirements, and over-banking tendencies.
2.  Selects an altitude recommended by the manufacturer, training syllabus, or other training directive, but in no case lower than 3,000 feet AGL.
3.  Establishes the recommended entry airspeed.
4.  Rolls into a coordinated turn of 180° or 360° with a bank of at least 45°. Maintains the bank angle within ±5° while in smooth, stabilized flight.
5.  Applies smooth coordinated pitch, bank, and power to maintain the specified altitude within ±100 feet and the desired airspeed within ±10 knots.
6.  Rolls out of the turn (at approximately the same rate as used to roll into the turn) within ±10° of the entry or specified heading, stabilizes the airplane in a straight-and-level attitude or, at the discretion of the examiner, reverses the direction of turn and repeats the maneuver in the opposite direction.
7.  Avoids any indication of an approaching stall, abnormal flight attitude, or exceeding any structural or operating limitation during any part of the maneuver.

## Task B: Approaches to Stalls and Stall Recovery

*References: 14 CFR part 61; FAA-H-8083-3; FSB Report; POH/AFM.*

**Three** approaches to stall are required, as follows (unless otherwise specified by the FSB Report):

1.  One in the takeoff configuration (except where the airplane uses only zero-flap takeoff configuration) or approach (partial) flap configuration
2.  One in a clean cruise configuration
3.  One in a landing configuration (landing gear and landing flaps set)

**CAUTION:** *Avoid deep stalls which are termed as "virtually unrecoverable" in airplanes, and "tip stalls" in swept wing airplanes.*

One of these approaches to a stall must be accomplished while in a turn using a bank angle of 15 to 30°.

**NOTE:** *When published, the aircraft manufacturer's procedures for the specific make/model/series airplane take precedent over the identification and recovery actions herein. One of these approaches to a stall must be accomplished while in a turn with a bank angle of 15 to 30°. If installed, one of these approaches to a stall should be accomplished by commands to the autopilot.*

**Objective:** To determine that the applicant:

1. In actual or simulated instrument conditions exhibits satisfactory knowledge of the factors, which influence stall characteristics, including the use of various drag configurations, power settings, pitch attitudes, weights, and bank angles. Also, demonstrates adequate knowledge of and skill in the proper procedure for resuming normal flight.

2. If accomplished in an airplane, selects an entry altitude that is in accordance with the AFM or POH, but in no case lower than an altitude that will allow recovery to be safely completed at a minimum of 3,000 feet AGL for non-transport certificated airplanes and 5,000 feet for transport certificated airplanes. When accomplished in an FSTD, the entry should be consistent with expected operational environment for the stall configuration with no minimum entry altitude defined.

3. Observes the area is clear of other aircraft prior to accomplishing an approach to a stall.

4. While maintaining the briefed profile, either manually or with the autopilot engaged, smoothly adjust pitch attitude, bank angle, and/or power setting that will induce a stall.

5. Announces the first indication of an impending stall (such as buffeting, stick shaker, decay of control effectiveness, and any other cues related to the specific airplane design characteristics) and promptly initiates recovery by disconnecting autopilot, reducing the angle of attack, leveling the wings, increasing power as necessary, and retracting any speedbrakes/spoilers to effect a safe and timely recovery.

*NOTE:* *If accomplished in an airplane in actual flight, the power should be set in accordance with the evaluator's instructors, when a limitation of power application is prudent for operational considerations and safety is not impaired.*

6. Regains control of the airplane and recovers to maneuvering speed and flight path appropriate for the airplane's configuration without exceeding the airplane's limitations or losing excessive altitude consistent with the airplane's performance capabilities. This should include reducing pitch attitude as necessary, reducing bank angle and adding power (no particular order implied!) to recover to missed approach or cruise configuration, airspeed and altitude. Some altitude loss is expected during the recovery, but re-establishment of controlled flight is paramount.

*NOTE:* *Evaluation criteria for a recovery from an approach to stall should not mandate a predetermined value for altitude loss and should not mandate maintaining altitude during recovery. Valid evaluation criteria must take into account the multitude of external (such as density altitude) and internal variables (ie. airplane mass, drag configuration and powerplant response time) which affect the recovery altitude.*

7. Demonstrates smooth, positive control during entry, approach to a stall, and recovery.

## Task C: *Powerplant Failure—Multiengine Airplane*

*References: 14 CFR part 61; POH/AFM.*

*NOTE:* *The feathering of one propeller and engine shutdown must be demonstrated in any multiengine airplane (or simulator/qualified FTD) equipped with propellers (includes turboprop), unless the airplane is an exception by the type rating and airplane certification (see page 13 of this document). The propeller must be safely feathered and unfeathered while airborne. In a multiengine jet airplane (or simulator/qualified FTD), one engine must be shut down and a restart must be demonstrated while airborne. Feathering or shutdown should be performed only under conditions and at such altitudes (no lower than 3,000 feet AGL) and in a position where a safe landing can be made on an established airport in the event difficulty is encountered in unfeathering the propeller or restarting the engine. At an altitude lower than 3,000 feet AGL, simulated engine failure will be performed by setting the powerplant controls to simulate zero-thrust. In the event the propeller cannot be unfeathered or the engine air started during the test, it should be treated as an emergency.*

*When authorized and conducted in a flight simulator, feathering or shutdown may be performed in conjunction with any procedure or maneuver and at locations and altitudes at the discretion of the examiner. However, when conducted in an FTD, authorizations are limited to shutdown, feathering, restart, and/or unfeathering procedures only. See appendix 1.*

**Objective:**   To determine that the applicant:

1. Exhibits knowledge of the flight characteristics and controllability associated with maneuvering with powerplant(s) inoperative (as appropriate to the airplane).
2. Maintains positive airplane control. Establishes a bank of approximately 5°, if required, or as recommended by the manufacturer, to maintain coordinated flight, and properly trims for that condition.
3. Sets powerplant controls, reduces drag as necessary, correctly identifies and verifies the inoperative powerplant(s) after the failure (or simulated failure).
4. Maintains the operating powerplant(s) within acceptable operating limits.
5. Follows the prescribed airplane checklist or coordinates with crew to ensure completion of checklist items in a timely manner and as recommended by the manufacturer, and verifies the procedures for securing the inoperative powerplant(s).
6. Determines the cause for the powerplant(s) failure and if a restart is a viable option.
7. Maintains desired altitude within ±100 feet, when a constant altitude is specified and is within the capability of the airplane.
8. Maintains the desired airspeed within ±10 knots.
9. Maintains the desired heading within ±10° of the specified heading.
10. Demonstrates proper powerplant restart procedures (if appropriate) in accordance with FAA-approved procedure/ checklist or the manufacturer's recommended procedures and pertinent checklist items.

## Task D:   *Powerplant Failure—Single–Engine Airplane*

*References:   14 CFR part 61; FAA-H-8083-3; POH/AFM.*

**NOTE:**   *No simulated powerplant failure will be given by the examiner in an airplane when an actual touchdown cannot be safely completed, should it become necessary.*

**Objective:** To determine that the applicant:

1. Exhibits knowledge of the flight characteristics, approach and forced (emergency) landing procedures, and related procedures to use in the event of a powerplant failure (as appropriate to the airplane).
2. Maintains positive control throughout the maneuver.
3. Establishes and maintains the recommended best glide airspeed, ±5 knots, and configuration during a simulated powerplant failure.
4. Selects a suitable airport or landing area, which is within the performance capability of the airplane.
5. Establishes a proper flight pattern to the selected airport or landing area, taking into account altitude, wind, terrain, obstructions, and other pertinent operational factors.
6. Follows the emergency checklist items appropriate to the airplane to ensure completion of checklist items in a timely manner and as recommended by the manufacturer.
7. Determines the cause for the simulated powerplant failure (if altitude permits) and if a restart is a viable option.
8. Uses configuration devices, such as landing gear and flaps in a manner recommended by the manufacturer and/or approved by the FAA.

## Task E: Specific Flight Characteristics

*References: 14 CFR part 61; FSB Reports; POH/AFM.*

**Objective:** To determine that the applicant:

1. Exhibits satisfactory knowledge of specific flight characteristics appropriate to the specific airplane, as identified by FSB Reports, such as Dutch Rolls for certain aircraft.
2. Uses proper technique to enter into, operate within, and recover from specific flight situations.

## Task F: Recovery from Unusual Attitudes

*References: 14 CFR part 61; FSB Reports; FAA-H-8083-15; POH/AFM.*

**Objective:** To determine that the applicant:

1. Exhibits knowledge of recovery from unusual attitudes.
2. Recovers from nose-high banked and/or level unusual attitudes, using proper pitch, bank, and power techniques.
3. Recovers from nose-low banked and/or level unusual attitudes, using proper pitch, bank, and power techniques.

## V.    Instrument Procedures

*NOTE:*   *Tasks B through F are not required if the applicant holds a*
*private pilot or commercial pilot certificate and is seeking a*
*type rating limited to VFR.*

### Task A:   *Standard Terminal Arrival/Flight Management*
*System Procedures*

*References:*   *14 CFR part 61; POH/AFM; AIM; En Route Low and*
*High Altitude Charts; Profile Descent Charts;*
*STARs/FMSPs; Standard Instrument Approach*
*Procedure Charts (SIAP); FAA-H-8261-1; AC 61-134,*
*AC 90-100.*

**Objective:**   To determine that the applicant:

1.   In actual or simulated instrument conditions, exhibits
adequate knowledge of En Route Low and High Altitude
Charts, STARs/FMSPs, Instrument Approach Procedure
Charts (IAP), and related pilot and controller
responsibilities.
2.   Uses the current and appropriate navigation publications for
the proposed flight.
3.   Selects and correctly identifies all instrument references,
flight director and autopilot controls, displays, and
navigation and communications equipment associated with
the arrival.
4.   Performs the airplane checklist items or coordinates with
crew to ensure completion of checklist items appropriate to
the arrival in a timely manner and as recommended by the
manufacturer.
5.   Establishes communications with ATC, using proper
phraseology.
6.   Complies, in a timely manner, with all ATC clearances,
instructions, and restrictions. Advises ATC if unable to
comply with ATC clearances or instructions.
7.   Exhibits satisfactory knowledge of two-way communications
failure procedures.
8.   Intercepts, in a timely manner, all courses, radials, and
bearings appropriate to the procedure, route, ATC
clearance, or as directed by the examiner.
9.   Adheres to airspeed restrictions and adjustments required
by regulations, ATC, the POH, the AFM, or the examiner.
10.   Establishes, where appropriate, a rate of descent consistent
with the airplane operating characteristics and safety.
11.   Maintains the appropriate airspeed/V-speed within ±10
knots, but not less than $V_{REF}$, if applicable; heading ±10°;
altitude within ±100 feet; and accurately tracks radials,
courses, and bearings.

12. Complies with the provisions of the Profile Descent, STAR, and other arrival procedures, as appropriate.

## Task B: Holding

*References: 14 CFR part 61; POH/AFM; AIM; En Route Low and High Altitude Charts; STARs; FMSP; Standard Instrument Approach Procedure Charts (SIAP).*

**Objective:** To determine that the applicant:

1. In actual or simulated instrument conditions, exhibits knowledge of holding procedures for standard and nonstandard, published and nonpublished holding patterns. If appropriate, demonstrates satisfactory knowledge of holding endurance, including, but not necessarily limited to, fuel on board, fuel flow while holding, fuel required to alternate, etc.
2. Changes to the recommended holding airspeed appropriate for the airplane and holding altitude, so as to cross the holding fix at or below maximum holding airspeed.
3. Recognizes arrival at the clearance limit or holding fix.
4. Follows appropriate entry procedures for a standard, nonstandard, published, or nonpublished holding pattern.
5. Complies with ATC reporting requirements.
6. Uses the proper timing criteria required by the holding altitude and ATC or examiner's instructions.
7. Complies with the holding pattern leg length when a distance measuring equipment (DME) distance is specified.
8. Uses the proper wind-drift correction techniques to accurately maintain the desired radial, track, courses, or bearing.
9. Arrives over the holding fix as close as possible to the "expect further clearance" time.
10. Maintains the appropriate airspeed/V-speed within ±10 knots, altitude within ±100 feet, headings within ±10°; and accurately tracks radials, courses, and bearings.
11. Selects and correctly identifies required instrument navigation aids, flight director and autopilot controls, navigation equipment displays associated with the holding clearance and expected clearance, as appropriate.

*FAA-S-8081-5F*

## Task C: Precision Approaches (PA)

References: *14 CFR part 61; POH/AFM; AIM; Standard Instrument Approach Procedure Charts (SIAP); FAA-H-8261-1, FAA-H-8083-15.*

**NOTE:** *Two precision approaches, utilizing NAVAID equipment for centerline and glideslope guidance, must be accomplished in simulated or actual instrument conditions to DA/DH. At least one approach must be flown manually without the use of an autopilot. The second approach may be flown via the autopilot, if appropriate, and if the DA/DH altitude does not violate the authorized minimum altitude for autopilot operation. Manually flown precision approaches may use raw data displays or may be flight director assisted, at the discretion of the examiner.*

*If the aircraft is equipped with advanced flight instrument displays, the raw data approach should be flown by reference to the backup instrumentation as much as is possible with the airplane's configuration.*

*For multiengine airplanes at least one manually controlled precision approach must be accomplished with a simulated failure of one powerplant. The simulated powerplant failure should occur before initiating the final approach segment and must continue to touchdown or throughout the missed approach procedure. As the markings on localizer/glideslope indicators vary, a one-quarter scale deflection of either the localizer, or glide slope indicator is when it is displaced one-fourth of the distance that it may be deflected from the on glide slope or on localizer position.*

**NOTE:** *A stabilized approach is characterized by a constant angle, constant rate of descent approach profile ending near the touchdown point, where the landing maneuver begins.*

**NOTE:** *If the installed equipment and data base is current and qualified for IFR flight and LPV approaches, an LPV approach can be flown to demonstrate precision approach proficiency if the LPV DA is equal to or less than 300 feet HAT.*

**Objective:** To determine that the applicant:

1. Exhibits satisfactory knowledge of the precision instrument approach procedures with all engines operating, and with one engine inoperative.
2. Accomplishes the appropriate precision instrument approaches as selected by the examiner.

3. Establishes two-way communications with ATC using the proper communications phraseology and techniques, or, directs co-pilot/safety pilot to do so, as appropriate for the phase of flight or approach segment.
4. Complies, in a timely manner, with all clearances, instructions, and procedures.
5. Advises ATC anytime the applicant is unable to comply with a clearance.
6. Establishes the appropriate airplane configuration and airspeed/V-speed considering turbulence, wind shear, microburst conditions, or other meteorological and operating conditions.
7. Completes the airplane checklist items or coordinates with crew to ensure completion of checklist items in a timely manner and as recommended by the manufacturer, appropriate to the phase of flight or approach segment, including engine out approach and landing checklists, if appropriate.
8. Prior to beginning the final approach segment, maintains the desired altitude ±100 feet, the desired airspeed within ±10 knots, the desired heading within ±5°; and accurately tracks radials, courses, and bearings.
9. Selects, tunes, identifies, and monitors the operational status of ground and airplane navigation equipment used for the approach, or correctly programs and monitors the RNAV equipment to display the proper course/track.
10. Applies the necessary adjustments to the published DA/DH and visibility criteria for the airplane approach category as required, such as—

    a. Notices to Airmen, including Flight Data Center (FDC) Procedural NOTAMs.
    b. Inoperative airplane and ground navigation equipment.
    c. Inoperative visual aids associated with the landing environment.
    d. National Weather Service (NWS) reporting factors and criteria.

11. Establishes a predetermined rate of descent at the point where the electronic glideslope begins, which approximates that required for the airplane to follow the glideslope.
12. Maintains a stabilized final approach, from the precision final approach fix to DA/DH, allowing no more than one-quarter scale deflection of either the glideslope or localizer indications, and maintains the desired airspeed within ±5 knots.
13. A missed approach or transition to a landing must be initiated at DA/DH.

14. Immediately initiates and executes the missed approach when at the DA/DH, if the required visual references for the runway are not unmistakably visible and identifiable.
15. Transitions to a normal landing approach (missed approach for seaplanes) only when the airplane is in a position from which a descent to a landing on the runway can be made at a normal rate of descent using normal maneuvering.
16. Maintains localizer and glide slope within one-quarter-scale deflection of the indicators during the visual descent from DA/DH to a point over the runway where the glideslope must be abandoned to accomplish a normal landing.

## Task D: Nonprecision Approaches (NPA)

References: 14 CFR part 61; POH/AFM; AIM; Standard Instrument Approach Procedure Charts (SIAP); FAA-H-8261-1, FAA-H-8083-15; AC 90-94.

**NOTE:** The applicant must accomplish at least two nonprecision approaches (one of which must include a procedure turn or, in the case of an RNAV approach, a Terminal Arrival Area (TAA) procedure) in simulated or actual weather conditions. At least one nonprecision approach must be flown without the use of autopilot and without the assistance of radar vectors. (The yaw damper and flight director are not considered parts of the autopilot for purpose of this part). The examiner will select nonprecision approaches that are representative of the type that the applicant is likely to use. The choices must utilize two different types of navigational aids. Some examples of navigational aids for the purpose of this part are: NDB, VOR, LOC, LDA, GPS, or RNAV.

**NOTE:** One approach should be flown with reference to backup or "fail down" instrumentation or navigation display depending on the aircraft's avionics configuration.

**NOTE:** The requirements for conducting a GPS approach for the purpose of this test are explained on pages 13 and 14 of the Introduction.

**Objective:** To determine that the applicant:

1. Exhibits adequate knowledge of nonprecision approach procedures representative of those the applicant is likely to use.
2. Accomplishes the nonprecision instrument approaches selected by the examiner.
3. Establishes two-way communications with ATC as appropriate to the phase of flight or approach segment and uses proper communications phraseology and techniques.
4. Complies with all clearances issued by ATC.

5. Advises ATC or the examiner any time the applicant is unable to comply with a clearance.
6. Establishes the appropriate airplane configuration and airspeed, and completes all applicable checklist items or coordinates with crew to ensure completion of checklist items in a timely manner and as recommended by the manufacturer.
7. Maintains, prior to beginning the final approach segment, the desired altitude ±100 feet, the desired airspeed ±10 knots, the desired heading ±5°; and accurately tracks radials, courses, and bearings.
8. Selects, tunes, identifies, and monitors the operational status of ground and airplane navigation equipment used for the approach.
9. Applies the necessary adjustments to the published Minimum Descent Altitude (MDA) and visibility criteria for the airplane approach category when required, such as—

   a. Notices to Airmen, including Flight Data Center Procedural NOTAMs.
   b. Inoperative airplane and ground navigation equipment.
   c. Inoperative visual aids associated with the landing environment.
   d. National Weather Service (NWS) reporting factors and criteria.

10. Establishes a rate of descent that will ensure arrival at the MDA (at, or prior to reaching, the visual descent point (VDP), if published) with the airplane in a position from which a descent from MDA to a landing on the intended runway can be made at a normal rate using normal maneuvering.
11. Allows, while on the final approach segment, not more than quarter-scale deflection of the Course Deviation Indicator (CDI) or ±5° in the case of the RMI or bearing pointer, and maintains airspeed within ±5 knots of that desired.
12. Maintains the MDA, when reached, within −0, +50 feet to the missed approach point.
13. Executes the missed approach at the missed approach point if the required visual references for the intended runway are not unmistakably visible and identifiable at the missed approach point.
14. Executes a normal landing from a straight-in or circling approach when instructed by the examiner.

## Task E: Circling Approach

*References: 14 CFR part 61; POH/AFM; AIM; Standard Instrument Approach Procedure Charts (SIAP); FAA-H-8261-1, FAA-H-8083-15.*

**Applicant NOTE:** *Expect this task to be combined with other tasks to include Area VI, Task C.*

**Objective:** To determine that the applicant:

1. Exhibits satisfactory knowledge of circling approach categories, speeds, and procedures to a specified runway.

2. In simulated or actual instrument conditions to MDA, accomplishes the circling approach selected by the examiner.

3. Demonstrates sound judgment and knowledge of the airplane maneuvering capabilities throughout the circling approach.

4. Confirms the direction of traffic and adheres to all restrictions and instructions issued by ATC.

5. Descends at a rate that ensures arrival at the MDA at, or prior to, a point from which a normal circle-to-land maneuver can be accomplished.

6. Avoids descent below the appropriate circling MDA or exceeding the visibility criteria until in a position from which a descent to a normal landing can be made.

7. Maneuvers the airplane, after reaching the authorized circling approach altitude, by visual references to maintain a flightpath that permits a normal landing on a runway that requires at least a 90° change of direction, from the final approach course, to align the aircraft for landing.

8. Performs the procedure without excessive maneuvering and without exceeding the normal operating limits of the airplane (the angle of bank should not exceed 30°).

9. Maintains the desired altitude within −0, +100 feet, heading/track within ±5°, the airspeed/V-speed within ±5 knots, but not less than the airspeed as specified in the POH or the AFM.

10. Uses the appropriate airplane configuration for normal and abnormal situations and procedures.

11. Turns in the appropriate direction, when a missed approach is dictated during the circling approach, and uses the correct procedure and airplane configuration.

12. Performs all procedures required for the circling approach and airplane control in a smooth, positive, and timely manner.

## Task F: *Missed Approach*

*References: 14 CFR part 61; POH/AFM; AIM; Standard Instrument Approach Procedure Charts (SIAP); FAA-H-8083-15, FAA-H-8261-1.*

**NOTE:** *The applicant must perform two missed approaches with one being from a precision approach (ILS, MLS, or GLS).*

*One complete published missed approach must be accomplished. Additionally, in multiengine airplanes, a missed approach must be accomplished with one engine inoperative (or simulated inoperative). The engine failure may be experienced any time prior to the initiation of the approach, during the approach, or during the transition to the missed approach attitude and configuration.*

*Descending below the MDA or continuing a precision approach below DH/DA as appropriate, unless the runway environment is in sight is considered unsatisfactory performance. However, even if the missed approach is properly initiated at DA/DH, most airplanes descend below DA/DH because of the momentum of the airplane transitioning from a stabilized approach to a missed approach. This descent below DA/DH is not considered unsatisfactory, as long as the precision approach was not continued below DA/DH.*

**Objective:**    To determine that the applicant:

1. Exhibits satisfactory knowledge of missed approach procedures associated with standard instrument approaches to include reference to standby (backup or fail down) instruments.
2. Initiates the missed approach procedure promptly by the timely application of power, establishes the proper climb attitude, and reduces drag in accordance with the approved procedures.
3. Reports to ATC, beginning the missed approach procedure.
4. Complies with the appropriate missed approach procedure or ATC clearance.
5. Advises ATC any time the applicant is unable to maneuver the airplane to comply with a clearance.
6. Follows the recommended airplane checklist items or coordinates with crew to ensure completion of checklist items in a timely manner and as recommended by the manufacturer appropriate to the go-around procedure for the airplane used.
7. Requests clearance, if appropriate, to the alternate airport, another approach, a holding fix, or as directed by the examiner.
8. Maintains the desired altitudes ±100 feet, airspeed ±5 knots, heading ±5°; and accurately tracks courses, radials, and bearings.

## VI. Landings and Approaches to Landings

**NOTE:** *Notwithstanding the authorizations for the combining of maneuvers and for the waiver of maneuvers, the applicant must make at least three actual landings (one to a full stop). These landings must include the types listed in this Area of Operation; however, more than one type may be combined where appropriate (i.e., crosswind and landing from a precision approach or landing with simulated powerplant failure, etc.). For all landings, touch down at the aiming point markings - 250' to +500' or where there are no runway aiming point markings, 750' to 1,500' from the approach threshold of the runway. Deceleration to taxi speed (20 knots or less on dry pavement, 10 knots or less on contaminated pavement) should be demonstrated on at least one landing to within the calculated landing distance plus 25% for the actual conditions with the runway centerline between the main landing gear. At no time will the outcome of the rollout and subsequent taxi be in doubt. Go-arounds will incur no penalty if successful. "Successful" is defined as no surface contact except for the landing gear on the runway. An amphibian type rating must bear the limitation "Limited to Land" or "Limited to Sea," as appropriate, unless the applicant demonstrates proficiency in both land and sea operations.*

### Task A: Normal and Crosswind Approaches and Landings

*References: 14 CFR part 61; POH/AFM; FAA-H-8083-3.*

**NOTE:** *In an airplane with a single powerplant, unless the applicant holds a commercial pilot certificate, he or she must accomplish three accuracy approaches and spot landings from an altitude of 1,000 feet or less, with the engine power lever in idle and 180° of change in direction. The airplane must touch the ground in a normal landing attitude beyond and within 200 feet of a designated line or point on the runway. At least one landing must be from a forward slip.*

**Objective:** To determine that the applicant:

1. Exhibits satisfactory knowledge of normal and crosswind approaches and landings including recommended approach angles, airspeeds, V-speeds, configurations, performance limitations, wake turbulence, LAHSO, and safety factors (as appropriate to the airplane).

2. Establishes the approach and landing configuration appropriate for the runway and meteorological conditions, and adjusts the powerplant controls as required.
3. Maintains a ground track that ensures the desired traffic pattern will be flown, taking into account any obstructions and ATC or examiner instructions.
4. Verifies existing wind conditions, makes proper correction for drift, and maintains a precise ground track.
5. Maintains a stabilized approach and the desired airspeed/ V-speed within ±5 knots.
6. Accomplishes a smooth, positively controlled transition from final approach to touchdown.
7. Maintains positive directional control and crosswind correction during the after-landing roll.
8. Uses spoilers, prop reverse, thrust reverse, wheel brakes, and other drag/braking devices, as appropriate, in such a manner to bring the airplane to a safe stop.
9. Completes the applicable after-landing checklist items or coordinates with crew to ensure completion of checklist items in a timely manner and as recommended by the manufacturer.

## Task B:  Landing from a Precision Approach

References:  14 CFR part 61; POH/AFM; AIM; FAA-H-8083-15.

**NOTE:** If circumstances beyond the control of the applicant prevent an actual landing, the examiner may accept an approach to a point where, in his or her judgment, a safe landing and a full stop could have been made, and credit given for a missed approach. Where a simulator approved for landing from a precision approach is used, the approach may be continued through the landing and credit given for one of the landings required by this Area of Operation.

**Applicant NOTE:**     Expect other tasks to be combined with this task (to include Area VI, Task C for multiengine airplanes).

**Objective:**   To determine that the applicant:

1. Exhibits awareness of landing in sequence from a precision approach.
2. Considers factors to be applied to the approach and landing such as displaced thresholds, meteorological conditions, NOTAMs, and ATC or examiner instructions.
3. Uses the airplane configuration and airspeed/V-speeds, as appropriate.
4. Maintains, during the final approach segment, glide slope and localizer indications within applicable standards of

deviation, and the recommended airspeed/V-speed ±5 knots.

5. Applies gust/wind factors as recommended by the manufacturer, and takes into account meteorological phenomena such as wind shear, microburst, and other related safety of flight factors.

6. Accomplishes the appropriate checklist items or coordinates with crew to ensure timely completion of checklist items in a timely manner and as recommended by the manufacturer or approved method.

7. Transitions smoothly from simulated instrument meteorological conditions (IMC) at a point designated by the examiner, maintaining positive airplane control.

8. Accomplishes a smooth, positively controlled transition from final approach to touchdown.

9. Maintains positive directional control and crosswind correction during the after-landing roll.

10. Uses spoilers, prop reverse, thrust reverse, wheel brakes, and other drag/braking devices, as appropriate, in such a manner to bring the airplane to a safe stop after landing.

11. Accomplishes the appropriate after-landing checklist items or coordinates with crew to ensure completion of after-landing checklist items in a timely manner and as recommended by the manufacturer.

## Task C: Approach and Landing with (Simulated) Powerplant Failure—Multiengine Airplane

*References: 14 CFR part 61; POH/AFM; FAA-H-8083-3.*

**NOTE:** *In airplanes with three powerplants, the applicant must follow a procedure (if approved) that approximates the loss of two powerplants, the center and one outboard powerplant. In other multiengine airplanes, the applicant must follow a procedure, which simulates the loss of 50 percent of available powerplants, the loss being simulated on one side of the airplane.*

**Applicant NOTE:** *Expect task to be combined with other tasks (to include Area V, Task E). May be limited by aircraft parameters under ambient conditions at examiner's discretion.*

**Objective:** To determine that the applicant:

1. Exhibits satisfactory knowledge of the flight characteristics and controllability associated with maneuvering to a landing with powerplant(s) inoperative (or simulated inoperative) including the controllability factors associated with maneuvering, and the applicable emergency procedures.

2. Maintains positive airplane control. Establishes a bank of approximately 5°, if required, or as recommended by the manufacturer, to maintain coordinated flight, and properly trims for that condition.
3. Sets powerplant controls, reduces drag as necessary, correctly identifies and verifies the inoperative powerplant(s) after the failure (or simulated failure).
4. Maintains the operating powerplant(s) within acceptable operating limits.
5. Follows the prescribed airplane checklist or coordinates with crew to ensure timely completion of checklist items in a timely manner and as recommended by the manufacturer, and verifies the procedures for securing the inoperative powerplant(s).
6. Proceeds toward the nearest suitable airport.
7. Maintains, prior to beginning the final approach segment, the desired altitude ±100 feet, the desired airspeed ±10 knots, the desired heading ±5°; and accurately tracks courses, radials, and bearings.
8. Establishes the approach and landing configuration appropriate for the runway or landing area, and meteorological conditions; and adjusts the powerplant controls as required.
9. Maintains a stabilized approach and the desired airspeed/ V-speed within ±5 knots.
10. Accomplishes a smooth, positively controlled transition from final approach to touchdown.
11. Maintains positive directional control and crosswind corrections during the after-landing roll.
12. Uses spoilers, prop reverse, thrust reversers, wheel brakes, and other drag/braking devices, as appropriate, in such a manner to bring the airplane to a safe stop after landing.
13. Accomplishes the appropriate after-landing checklist items or coordinates with crew to ensure completion of after-landing checklist items in a timely manner and as recommended by the manufacturer.

## Task D: Landing From a Circling Approach

*References: 14 CFR part 61; POH/AFM; AIM; FAA-H-8083-15.*

**APPLICANT NOTE:** *Expect task to be combined with other tasks (to include previous task, Task C for multiengine aircraft.)*

**Objective:** To determine that the applicant:

1. Exhibits knowledge of a landing from a circling approach.
2. Selects, and complies with, a circling approach procedure to a specified runway.

3. Considers the environmental, operational, and meteorological factors, which affect a landing from a circling approach.
4. Confirms the direction of traffic and adheres to all restrictions and instructions issued by ATC.
5. Descends at a rate that ensures arrival at the MDA at, or prior to, a point from which a normal circle-to-land maneuver can    be accomplished.
6. Avoids descent below the appropriate circling MDA or exceeding the visibility criteria until in a position from which descent to a normal landing can be made.
7. Accomplishes the appropriate checklist items or coordinates with crew to ensure completion of checklist items in a timely manner and as recommended by the manufacturer or approved method.
8. Maneuvers the airplane, after reaching the authorized circling approach altitude, by visual references, to maintain a flightpath that requires at least a 90° change of direction, from the final approach course, to align the aircraft for landing.
9. Performs the maneuver without excessive maneuvering and without exceeding the normal operating limits of the airplane. The angle of bank should not exceed 30°.
10. Maintains the desired altitude within +100, −0 feet, heading within ±5°, and approach airspeed/V-speed within ±5 knots.
11. Uses the appropriate airplane configuration for normal and abnormal situations and procedures.
12. Performs all procedures required for the circling approach and airplane control in a timely, smooth, and positive manner.
13. Accomplishes a smooth, positively controlled transition to final approach and touchdown or to a point where in the opinion of the examiner that a safe full stop landing could be made.
14. Maintains positive directional control and crosswind correction during the after-landing roll.
15. Uses spoilers, prop reverse, thrust reverse, wheel brakes, and other drag/braking devices, as appropriate, in such a manner to bring the airplane to a safe stop.
16. Accomplishes the appropriate after-landing checklist items or coordinates with crew to ensure completion of after-landing checklist items in a timely manner and as recommended by the manufacturer, after clearing the runway in a timely manner and as recommended by the manufacturer.

## Task E:   Rough Water Approach and Landing (AMES/ASES)

*References: POH/AFM; FAA-H-8083-3, FAA-H-8083-23.*

**NOTE:** *If a rough water condition does not exist, the applicant's knowledge of rough water elements must be evaluated through oral testing. The applicant's skill must be evaluated by simulating the Task.*

**Objective:** To determine that the applicant:

1. Exhibits knowledge of the elements related to a rough water approach and landing.
2. Considers the wind conditions, surrounding terrain, water depth, debris, and other watercraft.
3. Selects a suitable approach direction and touchdown area.
4. Establishes the recommended approach and landing configuration and adjusts power and pitch attitude as required.
5. Ensures that the landing gear and water rudders are retracted, if applicable.
6. Maintains a stabilized approach and recommended airspeed with gust factor applied, ±5 knots.
7. Contacts the water at the correct pitch attitude and touchdown speed.
8. Makes smooth, timely, and correct power and control application during the landing while remaining alert for a go-around should conditions be too rough.
9. Maintains positive after-landing control.
10. Completes appropriate checklists or coordinates with crew to ensure completion of after-landing checklist items in a timely manner and as recommended by the manufacturer or approved method.

### Task F: Glassy Water Approach And Landing (AMES/ASES)

*References: POH/AFM; FAA-H-8083-3, FAA-H-8083-23.*

**NOTE:** *If a glassy water condition does not exist, the applicant's satisfactory knowledge of glassy water elements must be evaluated through oral testing. The applicant's skill must be evaluated by simulating the Task.*

**Objective:** To determine that the applicant:

1. Exhibits satisfactory knowledge of the elements related to a glassy water approach and landing.
2. Considers the surrounding terrain, visual attitude references, water depth, debris, and other watercraft.
3. Selects a suitable approach path and touchdown area.
4. Ensures that the landing gear and water rudders are retracted, if applicable.

5.   Establishes the recommended approach and landing configuration and adjusts power and pitch attitude as required.
6.   Maintains a slightly nose-high stabilized approach at the recommended airspeed, ±5 knots and descent rate from last altitude reference, until touchdown.
7.   Makes smooth, timely, and correct power and control adjustments to maintain proper attitude and rate of descent to touchdown.
8.   Contacts the water at the correct pitch attitude and slows to idle taxi speed.
9.   Completes appropriate checklists or coordinates with crew to ensure completion of checklist items in a timely manner and as recommended by the manufacturer.

## Task G:   Confined-Area Approach and Landing (AMES/ASES)

References:   POH/AFM; FAA-H-8083-3, FAA-H-8083-23.

**NOTE:**   *This Task simulates an approach and landing to a small pond, which would require a spiral approach, wings level landing, and step turn upon landing; and a straight ahead approach and landing to a narrow waterway with obstructions at either end. The examiner must evaluate both landing situations for this Task.*

**Objective:**   To determine that the applicant:

1.   Exhibits knowledge of the elements related to a confined-area approach and landing.
2.   Considers the wind conditions, surrounding terrain, surface condition, water depth, debris, and other watercraft.
3.   Selects a suitable approach path and touchdown area.
4.   Establishes the recommended approach and landing configuration and airspeed, and adjusts pitch attitude and power as required.
5.   Ensures that the landing gear and water rudders are retracted, if applicable.
6.   Maintains a stabilized approach and recommended approach airspeed with gust factor applied, ±5 knots.
7.   Makes smooth, timely, and correct power and control application during the roundout and touchdown.
8.   Touches down smoothly at the recommended airspeed and pitch attitude, beyond and within 100 feet of a specified point/area.
9.   Maintains crosswind correction and directional control throughout the approach and landing.

10.  Completes appropriate checklists or coordinates with crew to ensure completion of checklist items in a timely manner and as recommended by the manufacturer.

## Task H:  Rejected Landing

References:   14 CFR part 61; AIM; POH/AFM; FSB Report; FAA-H-8083-3.

**NOTE:**  *The maneuver may be combined with instrument, circling, or missed approach procedures, but instrument conditions need not be simulated below 100 feet above the runway. This maneuver should be initiated approximately 50 feet above the runway or landing area and approximately over the runway threshold or as recommended by the FSB Report.*

*For those applicants seeking a VFR only type rating in an airplane not capable of instrument flight, and where this maneuver is accomplished with a simulated engine failure, it should not be initiated at speeds or altitudes below that recommended in the POH.*

**Objective:**   To determine that the applicant:

1.  Exhibits satisfactory knowledge of a rejected landing procedure including the conditions that dictate a rejected landing, the importance of a timely decision, LAHSO considerations, the recommended airspeed/V-speeds, and also the applicable "clean-up" procedure.
2.  Makes a timely decision to reject the landing for actual or simulated circumstances and makes appropriate notification when safety-of-flight is not an issue.
3.  Applies the appropriate power setting for the flight condition and establishes a pitch attitude necessary to obtain the desired performance.
4.  Retracts the wing flaps/drag devices and landing gear, if appropriate, in the correct sequence and at a safe altitude, establishes a positive rate of climb and the appropriate airspeed/V-speed within ±5 knots.
5.  Trims the airplane as necessary, and maintains the proper ground track during the rejected landing procedure.
6.  Accomplishes the appropriate after-landing checklist items or coordinates with crew to ensure timely completion of checklist items, in accordance with approved procedures.
7.  Reports reject to ATC in a timely manner, after executing reject procedures.

## Task I:  Landing from a No Flap or a Nonstandard Flap Approach

References:   14 CFR part 61; FSB Report; POH/AFM; FAA-H-8083-3.

**NOTE:** *This maneuver need not be accomplished for a particular airplane type if the Administrator has determined that the probability of flap extension failure on that type airplane is extremely remote due to system design. The examiner must determine whether checking on slats only and partial-flap approaches are necessary for the practical test. However, probability of asymmetrical flap failures should be considered in this making this determination.*

**Objective:**   To determine that the applicant:

1. Exhibits knowledge of the factors, which affect the flight characteristics of an airplane when full or partial flaps, leading edge flaps, and other similar devices become inoperative.
2. Uses the correct airspeeds/V-speeds for the approach and landing.
3. Maintains the proper airplane pitch attitude and flightpath for the configuration, gross weight, surface winds, and other applicable operational considerations.
4. Uses runway of sufficient length for the zero or nonstandard flap condition.
5. Maneuvers the airplane to a point where a touchdown at an acceptable point on the runway and a safe landing to a full stop could be made.
6. After landing, uses spoilers, prop reverse, thrust reverse, wheel brakes, and other drag/braking devices, as appropriate, in such a manner to bring the airplane to a safe stop.

# VII. Normal and Abnormal Procedures

## Task A: Normal and Abnormal Procedures

*References: 14 CFR part 61; POH/AFM; FSB Report.*

**Objective:** To determine that the applicant:

1. Exhibits satisfactory knowledge of the normal and abnormal procedures of the systems, subsystems, and devices relative to the airplane type (as may be determined by the examiner); knows immediate action items to accomplish, if appropriate, and proper checklist to accomplish or to call for, if appropriate.

2. Demonstrates the proper use of the airplane systems, subsystems, and devices (as may be determined by the examiner) appropriate to the airplane, such as—

    a. powerplant
    b. fuel system
    c. electrical system
    d. hydraulic system
    e. environmental and pressurization systems
    f. fire detection and extinguishing systems
    g. navigation and avionics systems to include backup (fail down) modes and procedures
    h. automatic flight control system, electronic flight instrument   system, and related subsystems to include backup (fail down) modes and procedures
    i. flight control systems
    j. anti-ice and deice systems
    k. airplane and personal emergency equipment
    l. other systems, subsystems, and devices specific to the type airplane, including make, model, and series

## VIII. Emergency Procedures

### Task A: Emergency Procedures

*References: 14 CFR part 61; POH/AFM.*

**Objective:** To determine that the applicant:

1. Exhibits satisfactory knowledge of the emergency procedures (as may be determined by the examiner) relating to the particular airplane type.
2. Demonstrates the proper emergency procedures (as must be determined by the examiner) relating to the particular airplane type, such as—

   a. emergency descent (maximum rate)
   b. inflight fire and smoke removal
   c. rapid decompression
   d. emergency evacuation
   e. airframe icing
   f. others (as may be required by the AFM)

3. Demonstrates the proper procedure for any other emergency outlined (as determined by the examiner) in the appropriate approved AFM to include demonstration of flight by reference to standby flight instruments.

# IX. Postflight Procedures

## Task A: After-Landing Procedures

*Reference: POH/AFM.*

**Objective:** To determine that the applicant:

1. Exhibits knowledge of safe after-landing, taxi, ramping, anchoring, docking, and mooring procedures, as appropriate.
2. Exhibits procedures to ensure the pilot maintains strict focus on the movement of the aircraft and ATC communications.
3. Demonstrates proficiency by maintaining correct and positive control. In airplanes equipped with float devices, this includes water taxiing, approaching a buoy, sailing, and docking.
4. Utilizes procedures for holding the pilot's workload to a minimum during taxi operations.
5. Maintains proper spacing on other aircraft, obstructions, and persons.
6. Utilizes taxi operation planning procedures, such as recording taxi instructions, reading back taxi clearances, and reviewing taxi routes on the airport diagram.
7. Utilizes procedures to ensure that clearance or instructions that are actually received are adhered to rather than the ones expected to be received.
8. Demonstrates procedures for briefing if a landing rollout to a taxiway exit will place the pilot in close proximity to another runway which can result in a runway incursion.
9. Accomplishes the applicable checklist items or coordinates with crew to ensure completion of checklist items in a timely manner and as recommended by the manufacturer and performs the recommended procedures.
10. Conducts appropriate after-landing/taxi procedures in the event the aircraft is on a taxiway that is between parallel runways.
11. Demonstrates specific procedures for operations at an airport with an operating air traffic control tower, with emphasis on ATC communications and runway entry/crossing authorizations.
12. Demonstrates and explains ATC communications and pilot actions before landing, and after landing at airports.
13. Maintains the desired track and speed.

14. Complies with instructions issued by ATC (or the examiner simulating ATC).
15. Observes runway hold lines, localizer and glide slope critical areas, and other surface control markings and lighting to prevent a runway incursion.
16. Maintains constant vigilance and airplane control during the taxi operation.
17. Demonstrates and/or explains procedural differences for night operations.
18. Demonstrates and explains the use(s) of aircraft exterior lighting and differences for day and night operations.
19. Explains and discusses the hazards of low visibility operations.

## Task B: Anchoring (AMES/ASES)

References: POH/AFM; FAA-H-8083-3, FAA-H-8083-23.

**Objective:** To determine that the applicant:

1. Exhibits knowledge of the elements related to anchoring in lakes, rivers, and tidal areas.
2. Selects a suitable area for anchoring considering seaplane movement, water depth, tides, wind, and weather changes.
3. Uses an adequate number of anchors and lines of sufficient strength and length to ensure the seaplane's security.

## Task C: Docking and Mooring (AMES/ASES)

References: POH/AFM; FAA-H-8083-3, FAA-H-8083-23.

**Objective:** To determine that the applicant:

1. Exhibits knowledge of the elements related to docking or mooring.
2. Approaches the dock or mooring buoy in the proper direction considering speed, hazards, wind, and water current.
3. Ensures seaplane security.

## Task D: Beaching (AMES/ASES)

References: POH/AFM; FAA-H-8083-3, FAA-H-8083-23.

**Objective:** To determine that the applicant:

1. Exhibits knowledge of the elements related to beaching.
2. Selects a suitable area for beaching, considering water depth, current, tide, and wind.
3. Approaches from the proper direction and at a suitable speed for the beach condition.

4. Beaches and secures the seaplane in a manner that will protect it from harmful effects of wind, waves, and changes in water level.
5. Departs the beach in a safe manner, considering wind, current, traffic, and hazards.

## Task E: Ramping (AMES/ASES)

References: POH/AFM; FAA-H-8083-3, FAA-H-8083-23.

**Objective:** To determine that the applicant:

1. Exhibits knowledge of the elements related to ramping.
2. Approaches the ramp from the proper direction and at a safe speed, considering current, wind, and type of ramp.
3. Ramps the seaplane at the proper speed and attitude.
4. Secures the seaplane on the ramp in a manner that will protect it from the harmful effects of wind, waves, and changes of water level.
5. Departs the ramp in a manner that does not endanger other persons or watercraft in the area.
6. Re-enters the water.

## Task F: Parking and Securing

Reference: POH/AFM.

**Objective:** To determine that the applicant:

1. Demonstrates knowledge of the parking, and the securing airplane procedures.
2. Demonstrates knowledge of the airplane forms/logs to record the flight time/discrepancies.
3. Demonstrates knowledge of any installed and auxiliary aircraft security equipment, as appropriate.

**Appendix:**
**Task vs. Simulation Device Credit**

## Task vs. Simulation Device Credit

Examiners conducting the Airline Transport Pilot and Aircraft Type Rating Practical Test Standards—Airplane with simulation devices should consult appropriate documentation to ensure that the device has been approved for training, testing, and checking the Tasks in question. The documentation for each device should reflect that the following activities have occurred.

1. The device must be evaluated, determined to meet the appropriate standards, and assigned the appropriate qualification level by the National Simulator Program Manager. The device must continue to meet qualification standards through continuing evaluations as required in 14 CFR Part 60. Level 1, 2, and 3 devices may not be used to accomplish the maneuvers required by this PTS. For simulators, 14 CFR Part 60 or other applicable grandfathered standards for previously qualified FSTDs (as defined in § 60.17) will be used.
2. The FAA must approve the device for training, testing, and checking the specific Tasks listed in this appendix.
3. The device must continue to support the level of student or applicant performance required by this PTS.

**NOTE:** *Users of the following chart are cautioned that use of the chart alone is incomplete. The description and Objective of each Task as listed in the body of the PTS, including all NOTES, must also be incorporated for accurate simulation device use.*

## Use of Chart

X   Creditable
A   Creditable if appropriate systems are installed and operating

***NOTES:***

1. The airplane may be used for all Tasks.
2. Training Devices below Level 4 may **not** be used for airplane type ratings.
3. Standards for and use of Level 1 Flight Training Devices have not been determined.

FAA-S-8081-5F

## Task vs. Simulation Device Credit

| Flight Task Areas of Operation | 4 | 5 | 6 | 7 | A | B | C | D |
|---|---|---|---|---|---|---|---|---|
| **II. Preflight Procedures** | | | | | | | | |
| A. Preflight Inspection (Cockpit Only) | A | A | X | X | X | X | X | X |
| B. Powerplant Start | A | A | X | X | X | X | X | X |
| C. Taxiing | | | | | | | | |
| F. Pretakeoff Checks | A | A | X | X | X | X | X | X |
| **III. Takeoff and Departure Phase** | | | | | | | | |
| A. Normal and Crosswind Takeoff | – | – | X | X | X | X | X | X |
| E. Instrument Takeoff (levels 6 & 7 require a visual system approved in accordance with 14 CFR part 60) | – | – | A | A | A | X | X | X |
| F. Powerplant Failure During Takeoff | – | – | A | A | A | X | X | X |
| G. Rejected Takeoff (levels 6 & 7 require a visual system approved in accordance with 14 CFR part 60) | – | – | A | A | A | X | X | X |
| H. Departure Procedures | – | – | X | X | X | X | X | X |
| **IV. Inflight Maneuvers** | | | | | | | | |
| A. Steep Turns | – | – | X | X | X | X | X | X |
| B. Approaches to Stalls (Use of Levels 6 & 7 require operational synthetic stall warning system. Motion in an FSS should be used when a pilot needs to feel the stimulus and develop the recovery behaviors that rely on motion.) | – | – | X | X | X | X | X | X |
| C. Powerplant Failure – Multiengine Airplane | – | – | X | X | X | X | X | X |
| D. Powerplant Failure – Single-Engine Airplane | – | – | X | X | X | X | X | X |
| E. Specific Flight Characteristics and FSB Special Emphasis Items | *Level of device as determined by the airplane Flight Standardization Board (FSB).* | | | | | | | |
| F. Recovery from Unusual Attitudes | – | – | X | X | X | X | X | X |

## Task vs. Simulation Device Credit

| Flight Task Areas of Operation | Flight Simulation Device Level | | | | | | | |
|---|---|---|---|---|---|---|---|---|
| | 4 | 5 | 6 | 7 | A | B | C | D |
| **V. Instrument Procedures** | | | | | | | | |
| A. Standard Terminal Arrival/Flight Management System Procedures | – | – | X | X | X | X | X | X |
| B. Holding | – | – | X | X | X | X | X | X |
| C1. Precision Instrument Approach (All Engines Operating) (Autopilot/Manual Flt. Dir. Assist/Manual Raw Data) (Levels 2 & 5 use limited to A/P coupled approach only) | – | A | X | X | X | X | X | X |
| C2. Precision Instrument Approach (PA) (One Engine Inop.) (Manual Flt. Dir. Asst/Manual Raw Data) | – | – | – | – | X | X | X | X |
| D. Nonprecision Approaches (NPA) (Not more than 1 authorized in a device less than Level A simulator) (Levels 2 & 5 use limited to A/P coupled approach only) | – | A | X | X | X | X | X | X |
| E. Circling Approach (each approach must be specifically authorized) | – | – | – | – | X | X | X | X |
| F1. Missed Approach (Normal) | – | – | – | – | X | X | X | X |
| F2. Missed Approach (Powerplant Failure) | – | – | – | – | X | X | X | X |
| **VI. Landings and Approaches to Landings** | | | | | | | | |
| A. Normal and Crosswind Approaches and Landings | – | – | – | – | – | – | X | X |
| B. Landing from a Precision Approach (PA) | – | – | – | – | – | – | X | X |
| C. Approach and Landing With (Simulated) Powerplant Failure – Multiengine Airplane | – | – | – | – | – | – | X | X |
| D. Landing from Circling Approach | – | – | – | – | – | – | X | X |
| H. Rejected Landing | – | – | – | – | X | X | X | X |
| I. Landing from a No Flap or a Nonstandard Flap Approach | – | – | – | – | – | – | X | X |

FAA-S-8081-5F

## Task vs. Simulation Device Credit

| Flight Task Areas of Operation | 4 | 5 | 6 | 7 | A | B | C | D |
|---|---|---|---|---|---|---|---|---|
| **VII. Normal and Abnormal Procedures[23]** | | | | | | | | |
| A. Powerplant (including shutdown and restart) | A | A | X | X | X | X | X | X |
| B. Fuel System | A | A | X | X | X | X | X | X |
| C. Electrical System | A | A | X | X | X | X | X | X |
| D. Hydraulic System | A | A | X | X | X | X | X | X |
| E. Environmental and Pressurization Systems | A | A | X | X | X | X | X | X |
| F. Fire Protection and Extinguisher Systems | A | A | X | X | X | X | X | X |
| G. Navigation and Avionics Systems | A | A | X | X | X | X | X | X |
| H. Automatic Flight Control System, Electronic Flight Instrument System, and Related Subsystems | A | A | X | X | X | X | X | X |
| I. Flight Control Systems | A | A | X | X | X | X | X | X |
| J. Anti-ice and Deice Systems | – | A | A | X | X | X | X | X |
| K. Aircraft and Personal Emergency Equipment | A | A | X | X | X | X | X | X |
| L. Others, as determined by make, model, or series | A | A | X | X | X | X | X | X |
| **VIII. Emergency Procedures** | | | | | | | | |
| A. Emergency Descent (Max. Rate) | – | – | X | X | X | X | X | X |
| B. Inflight Fire and Smoke Removal | – | A | X | X | X | X | X | X |
| C. Rapid Decompression | – | – | X | X | X | X | X | X |
| D. Emergency Evacuation | – | A | X | X | X | X | X | X |
| E. Others (as may be required by AFM) | A | A | X | X | X | X | X | X |
| **IX. Postflight Procedures** | | | | | | | | |
| A. After-Landing Procedures | A | A | X | X | X | X | X | X |
| F. Parking and Securing | A | A | X | X | X | X | X | X |

[2] Evaluation of normal and abnormal procedures may be accomplished in conjunction with other events.

[3] Situations resulting in asymmetrical thrust or drag conditions (i.e., asymmetrical flight controls) must be accomplished in at least a Level A device. However, shutdown and restart (procedures only) may be accomplished in a properly equipped FTD.

U.S. Department
of Transportation

**Federal Aviation
Administration**

# FAA-S-8081-10D
## (with Change 1)

# Aircraft Dispatcher
# Practical Test Standards

# May 2013
## (effective August 1, 2013)

Flight Standards Service
Washington, DC 20591

*(this page intentionally left blank)*

# Aircraft Dispatcher
# Practical Test Standards

# 2013

Flight Standards Service
Washington, DC 20591

*(this page intentionally left blank)*

# Note

Material in FAA-S-8081-10D will be effective August 1, 2013. All
previous editions of the Aircraft Dispatcher Practical Test Standards
will be obsolete as of this date.

## Record of Changes

### Change 1 (11/7/2013)

- Added 14 CFR part 117 to reference list in Practical Test Book Description section of the Introduction (page 3).

  o This regulation becomes effective on January 4, 2014.

- Added 14 CFR part 117 to references for Area of Operation II, Task B: Airports, Crew, and Company Procedures (page 20).

## *Major Enhancements to Version FAA-S-8081-10D*

- Introduction
  - Revised "General Information" section
  - Revised title of "Practical Test Standards Concept" section (previously titled "Practical Test Standard Concept")
  - Revised "Practical Test Standards Description" section
  - Revised list of references

    - Removed AC 90-94: Guidelines for Using Global Positioning System Equipment for IFR En Route and Terminal Operations and for Nonprecision Instrument Approaches in the U.S. National Airspace System

    - Corrected the title for 49 CFR part 1544 to "Aircraft Operator Security: Air Carriers and Commercial Operators"

    - Added the following:

      - 14 CFR part 110: General Requirements

      - 14 CFR part 119: Certification: Air Carriers and Commercial Operators

      - 14 CFR part 120: Drug and Alcohol Testing Program

      - AC 90-105: Approval Guidance for RNP Operations and Barometric Vertical Navigation in the U.S. National Airspace System

      - AC 120-101: Air Carrier Operational Control

      - AFM: Airplane Flight Manual

    - Revised Note

  - Revised "Use of the Practical Test Standards Book" section (previously titled "Use of the Practical Test Standard Book")
  - Revised element 3 and removed element 8 in the "Special Emphasis Areas" section
  - Revised title and content of the "Aircraft Dispatcher Practical Test Prerequisites" section (previously titled "Practical Test Prerequisites")
  - Added "Aircraft Dispatcher Certification Prerequisites" section
  - Revised "Equipment and Documents Required for the Practical Test" section

- o Revised "Examiner Responsibility" section
- o Revised "Satisfactory Performance" section
- o Revised "Unsatisfactory Performance" section
- o Added "Notice of Disapproval" section
- o Revised "Letter of Discontinuance" section
- o Revised "Dispatch Resource Management (DRM)" section
- o Revised Aeronautical Decision Making and Risk Management" section

- Area of Operation I: Flight Planning/Dispatch Release

  - o Task A: Regulatory Requirements
    - Revised References
    - Revised Objective 2

  - o Task B: Meteorology
    - Revised References
    - Revised Objective 2

  - o Task C: Weather Observations, Analysis, and Forecasts
    - Revised References
    - Revised Note
    - Revised element *a* and added element *l* to Objective 1

  - o Task D: Weather-Related Hazards
    - Revised References
    - Revised Objective

  - o Task E: Aircraft Systems, Performance, and Limitations
    - Revised References

  - o Task F: Navigation and Aircraft Navigation Systems
    - Revised References
    - Revised element *b* of Objective 3

  - o Task G: Practical Dispatch Applications
    - Revised References

  - o Task H: Manuals, Handbooks, and Other Written Guidance
    - Revised References

- - Revised Objective
- Area of Operation II: Preflight, Takeoff, and Departure
  - Task A: Air Traffic Control Procedures
    - Revised References
    - Revised Objective 10
  - Task B: Airports, Crew, and Company Procedures
    - Revised References
- Area of Operation III: Inflight Procedures
  - Task A: Routing, Re-Routing, and Flight Plan Filing
    - Add Objective 4
  - Task B: En Route Communication Procedures and Requirements
    - Revised References
- Area of Operation V: Post-Flight Procedures
  - Task B: Flight Documentation\
    - Renamed Task (previously titled "Trip Records")
    - Revised Objective 1
- Area of Operation VI: Abnormal and Emergency Procedures
  - Task: Abnormal and Emergency Procedures
    - Revised References

*(this page intentionally left blank)*

# Foreword

The Aircraft Dispatcher Practical Test Standards book has been published by the Federal Aviation Administration (FAA) to establish the standards for the aircraft dispatcher certification practical test. Qualified FAA inspectors and designated dispatcher examiners shall conduct practical tests in compliance with these standards. Instructors and applicants should find these standards helpful in practical test preparation.

Signed: 05/06/2013

John Allen

Director, Flight Standards Service

*(this page intentionally left blank)*

# Table of Contents

**Introduction**

General Information .................................................................. 1
Practical Test Standards Concept ........................................... 1
Practical Test Standards Description ..................................... 2
Use of the Practical Test Standards Book .............................. 5
Special Emphasis Areas ........................................................... 6
Aircraft Dispatcher Practical Test Prerequisites ................. 6
Aircraft Dispatcher Certification Prerequisites ................... 7
Equipment and Documents Required for the Practical Test ....... 7
Examiner Responsibility .......................................................... 8
Satisfactory Performance ........................................................ 9
Unsatisfactory Performance ................................................... 9
Notice of Disapproval ............................................................ 10
Letter of Discontinuance ...................................................... 10
Dispatch Resource Management (DRM) ............................... 10
Aeronautical Decision Making and Risk Management ............. 11

**Areas of Operation**

I.  Flight Planning/Dispatch Release ......................................... 13

  Task A:  Regulatory Requirements ..................................... 13
  Task B:  Meteorology .......................................................... 13
  Task C:  Weather Observations, Analysis, and
           Forecasts ............................................................. 14
  Task D:  Weather-Related Hazards ..................................... 15
  Task E:  Aircraft Systems, Performance, and
           Limitations .......................................................... 15
  Task F:  Navigation and Aircraft Navigation Systems ........ 17
  Task G:  Practical Dispatch Applications ............................ 18
  Task H:  Manuals, Handbooks, and Other Written
           Guidance ............................................................. 18

II.  Preflight, Takeoff, and Departure ........................................ 20

  Task A:  Air Traffic Control Procedures .............................. 20
  Task B:  Airports, Crew, and Company Procedures ............ 20

III. Inflight Procedures ................................................................. 21

    Task A:   Routing, Re-Routing, and Flight Plan Filing ........... 21
    Task B:   En Route Communication Procedures and
               Requirements ......................................................... 21

IV. Arrival, Approach, and Landing Procedures ....................... 22

    Task:     ATC and Air Navigation Procedures ...................... 22

V. Post-Flight Procedures ........................................................... 23

    Task A:   Communication Procedures and
               Requirements ......................................................... 23
    Task B:   Flight Documentation ............................................ 23

VI. Abnormal and Emergency Procedures ................................. 24

    Task:     Abnormal and Emergency Procedures ................ 24

# Introduction

## General Information

The Flight Standards Service (AFS) of the Federal Aviation Administration (FAA) has developed these practical test standards as the standards that shall be used by qualified FAA inspectors and designated examiners when conducting the Aircraft Dispatcher Practical Test. Instructors are expected to use this book when preparing applicants for practical tests. Applicants should be familiar with this book and refer to these standards during their training.

Information considered directive in nature is described in these practical test standards (PTS) in terms such as "shall" and "must," indicating the actions are mandatory. Guidance information is described in terms such as "should" and "may," indicating the actions are desirable or permissive, but not mandatory.

The FAA gratefully acknowledges the valuable assistance provided by many individuals and organizations throughout the aviation community who contributed their time and talent in assisting with the revision of these practical test standards.

This PTS may be purchased from the Superintendent of Documents, U.S. Government Printing Office (GPO), Washington, DC 20402-9325, or from GPO's website at http://bookstore.gpo.gov.

This PTS is available for download, in pdf format, from www.faa.gov.

This PTS is published by the U.S. Department of Transportation, Federal Aviation Administration, Airman Testing Standards Branch, AFS-630, P.O. Box 25082, Oklahoma City, OK 73125.

Comments regarding this PTS may be sent to the following e-mail address:  AFS630comments@faa.gov.

## Practical Test Standards Concept

Title 14 of the Code of Federal Regulations (14 CFR) part 65 specifies the subject areas in which knowledge and skill must be demonstrated by the applicant before the issuance of an Aircraft Dispatcher Certificate. The CFRs provide the flexibility to permit the FAA to publish practical test standards containing the Areas of Operation and specific Tasks in which competency shall be demonstrated. The FAA will revise this book whenever it is determined that changes are needed in the interest of safety. *Adherence to provisions of the regulations and the practical*

***test standards is mandatory for the evaluation of aircraft
dispatcher applicants.***

## *Practical Test Standards Description*

This test book contains the Practical Test Standards for Aircraft
Dispatcher. The Aircraft Dispatcher Practical Test Standards
includes the Areas of Operation and Tasks for the initial issuance of
an Aircraft Dispatcher Certificate.

**Areas of Operation** are phases of the practical test arranged in a
logical sequence within the standard. They begin with Flight
Planning/Dispatch Release and end with Abnormal and Emergency
Procedures. The examiner, however, may conduct the practical test
in any sequence that will result in a complete and efficient test.

**Tasks** are titles of knowledge areas or procedures appropriate to an
Area of Operation.

**References** identify the publication(s) that describe(s) the Task.
Descriptions of Tasks are not included in these standards because
this information can be found in the current issue of the listed
reference. Publications other than those listed may be used for
references if their content conveys substantially the same meaning
as the referenced publications. Except where appropriate (e.g.,
pertinent CFRs), references listed in this document are NOT meant
to supersede or otherwise replace manufacturer or other FAA-
approved or accepted data. References are meant to serve as
general information and study material resources.

**Objectives** list the important elements that must be satisfactorily
performed to demonstrate competency in a Task.

**Note** is used to emphasize special considerations required in the
Area of Operation or Task.

The examiner determines that the applicant meets the Task
Objective through the demonstration of competency in all elements
of knowledge and/or skill unless otherwise noted. The Objectives of
the Tasks in certain Areas of Operation, such as arrival, approach,
and landing procedures, should include only knowledge elements.
Examiners may introduce common errors as part of the objectives in
a particular Task that includes elements of skill as well as
knowledge. In meeting the objectives, an applicant must be able to
describe, recognize, analyze, and correct the errors.

These practical test standards are based on the following references:

| | |
|---|---|
| **14 CFR part 1** | Definitions and Abbreviations |
| **14 CFR part 25** | Airworthiness Standards: Transport Category Airplanes |
| **14 CFR part 61** | Certification: Pilots, Flight Instructors, and Ground Instructors |
| **14 CFR part 65** | Certification: Airmen Other Than Flight Crewmembers |
| **14 CFR part 71** | Designation of Class A, B, C, D, and E Airspace Areas; Airways; Air Traffic Service; Routes; and Reporting Points |
| **14 CFR part 91** | General Operating and Flight Rules |
| **14 CFR part 110** | General Requirements |
| **14 CFR part 117** | Flight and Duty Limitations and Rest Requirements: Flightcrew Members |
| **14 CFR part 119** | Certification: Air Carriers and Commercial Operators |
| **14 CFR part 120** | Drug and Alcohol Testing Program |
| **14 CFR part 121** | Operating Requirements: Domestic, Flag, and Supplemental Operations |
| **14 CFR part 139** | Certification and Operations: Land Airports Serving Certain Air Carriers |
| **49 CFR part 175** | Hazardous Materials Regulations; Carriage by Aircraft |
| **49 CFR part 830** | Notification and Reporting of Aircraft Accidents or Incidents and Overdue Aircraft, and Preservation of Aircraft Wreckage, Mail, Cargo, and Records |
| **49 CFR part 1544** | Aircraft Operator Security: Air Carriers and Commercial Operators |
| **FAA-H-8083-1** | Aircraft Weight and Balance Handbook |
| **FAA-H-8083-15** | Instrument Flying Handbook |
| **FAA-H-8083-25** | Pilot's Handbook of Aeronautical Knowledge |
| **FAA-H-8261-1** | Instrument Procedures Handbook |
| **FAA Order 8260.3** | United States Standard for Terminal Instrument Procedures (TERPS) |
| **AC 00-2** | Advisory Circular Checklist |
| **AC 00-6** | Aviation Weather |
| **AC 00-45** | Aviation Weather Services |
| **AC 20-29** | Use of Aircraft Fuel Anti-Icing Additives |

| | |
|---|---|
| AC 20-117 | Hazards Following Ground Deicing and Ground Operations in Conditions Conducive to Aircraft Icing |
| AC 60-22 | Aeronautical Decision-Making |
| AC 60-28 | English Language Skill Standards Required by 14 CFR parts 61, 63, and 65 |
| AC 61-84 | Role of Preflight Preparation |
| AC 91-51 | Effect of Icing on Aircraft Control and Airplane Deice Anti-ice Systems |
| AC 91-74 | Pilot Guide Flight in Icing Conditions |
| AC 90-79 | Recommended Practices and Procedures for the Use of Long-Range Navigation |
| AC 90-91 | North American Route Program (NRP) |
| AC 90-105 | Approval Guidance for RNP Operations and Barometric Vertical Navigation in the U.S. National Airspace System |
| AC 91-43 | Unreliable Airspeed Indicators |
| AC 91-70 | Oceanic Operations |
| AC 120-27 | Aircraft Weight and Balance Control |
| AC 120-28 | Criteria for Approval of Category III Landing Weather Minima for Takeoff, Landing, and Rollout |
| AC 120-29 | Criteria for Approval of Category I and Category II Weather Minima for Approach |
| AC 120-57 | Surface Movement Guidance System |
| AC 120-60 | Ground Deicing and Anti-icing Program |
| AC 120-101 | Air Carrier Operational Control |
| AC 121-26 | Airports—Required Data |
| AC 121-32 | Dispatch Resource Management Training |
| A/FD | Airport/Facility Directory |
| AFM | Airplane Flight Manual |
| AIM | Aeronautical Information Manual |
| CDL | Configuration Deviation List |
| DP | Departure Procedure |
| IAP | Instrument Approach Procedure |
| IFIM | International Flight Information Manual |
| MEL | Minimum Equipment List |
| NOTAM | Notice to Airmen |
| ODP | Obstacle Departure Procedure |
| SID | Standard Instrument Departure Procedure |

| | |
|---|---|
| **STAR** | Standard Terminal Arrival Route |
| **Charts** | En Route High and Low Altitude Charts, Terminal Area Charts, Profile Descent Charts |
| **OpSpecs** | Operations Specifications |

**NOTE:** *The latest revision of the references must be used.*

## Use of the Practical Test Standards Book

The FAA requires that all Aircraft Dispatcher Practical Tests be conducted in accordance with the Aircraft Dispatcher Practical Test Standards and the policies set forth in the Introduction. Applicants must be evaluated in **all** Tasks included in each Area of Operation of the practical test standard unless otherwise noted.

When using the practical test book, the examiner must evaluate the applicant's knowledge and skill in sufficient depth to determine that the standards of performance listed for all Tasks are met. However, when a particular Element is not appropriate to the aircraft, its equipment, or operational capability, etc., that Element, at the discretion of the examiner, may be omitted. It is not intended that the examiner follow the precise order in which Areas of Operation and Tasks appear in the practical test standards. The examiner may change the sequence or combine Tasks with similar Objectives to conserve time.

In preparation for each practical test, the examiner shall develop a written "plan of action." The "plan of action" shall include all required Tasks in each Area of Operation. If the Elements in one Task have already been evaluated in another Task, they need not be repeated. For example, the "plan of action" need not include evaluating the applicant on hazardous weather conditions or NTSB reporting requirements at the end of the practical test if knowledge of that Element was sufficiently demonstrated at the beginning of the test. One or more scenarios may be used in testing the applicant. The "plan of action" should be written in the order that the evaluation will be conducted but maintain the flexibility to be changed due to unexpected situations as they arise. It must be complete enough to ensure that all the selected Tasks are evaluated. *Any Task selected for evaluation during a practical test shall be evaluated in its entirety.*

The Objectives of all Tasks must be demonstrated at some time during the practical test. It is of the utmost importance that the examiner accurately evaluates the applicant's ability to perform safely as an aircraft dispatcher.

In an automated environment, the examiner must require an applicant to demonstrate adequate knowledge and skill in manual flight planning and dispatch procedures. The preparation of a manual flight plan is mandatory during the practical test. In addition, an examiner may choose to have the applicant provide manual validation of a computer generated flight plan and dispatch release as a means to ensure the applicant is able to decipher and crosscheck computer-produced calculations.

## Special Emphasis Areas

Examiners shall place special emphasis upon areas that are most critical to dispatching and flight safety. Although these areas may not be shown under each Task, they are essential to flight safety and must receive careful evaluation throughout the practical test.

Among these are:

1. Positive Operational Control;
2. Aircraft Performance and Driftdown;
3. Weather Requirements for Departure/Destination and Alternates;
4. Hazardous Weather Awareness, Recognition and Avoidance;
5. Aeronautical Decision Making (ADM);
6. Risk Management Procedures (RMP);
7. Dispatcher Resource Management (DRM); and
8. Other areas deemed appropriate to any phase of the practical test.

## Aircraft Dispatcher Practical Test Prerequisites

To be eligible to take the Aircraft Dispatcher Practical Test, an applicant must meet the following criteria, as required by 14 CFR part 65:

1. Be at least 21 years of age;
2. Be able to read, speak, write, and understand the English Language;
3. Present documentary evidence of passing the required knowledge test prescribed by 14 CFR part 65.55 within the preceding 24 months; and
4. Comply with the experience or training requirements of 14 CFR part 65.57.

Applicants should expect the testing to require 4 to 6 hours to complete.

In accordance with the requirements of 14 CFR 65.53(b)(2) and ICAO aviation English Language proficiency requirements, the entire application process and testing procedures must be accomplished fluently enough in the English language such that crew coordination and communication is never in doubt.

If there are questions concerning English language requirements, refer to "AC 60-28, English Language Skill Standards Required by 14 CFR parts 61, 63, and 65."

## *Aircraft Dispatcher Certification Prerequisites*

To be eligible for an aircraft dispatcher certificate, an applicant must meet the following requirements:

1.   Be at least 23 years of age;

   a.   Applicants under 23 years of age that pass the practical test will receive a letter of aeronautical competency in accordance with FAA Order 8900.1 volume 13, chapter 3, section 4.

2.   Satisfy elements 2 through 4 from the "Aircraft Dispatcher Practical Test Prerequisites" section above; and
3.   Pass the required practical test prescribed by 14 CFR part 65.59.

## *Equipment and Documents Required for the Practical Test*

The examiner is responsible for supplying weather information and NOTAMs for the test when current weather information is not available.

Materials to be supplied by the applicant, as determined by the examiner, include the following:

1.   Airplane Flight Manual;
2.   General Operating Manual;
3.   Operations Specifications (may be included in the General Operating Manual;
4.   En Route Low/High Altitude Charts;
5.   Standard Instrument Departures;
6.   Standard Terminal Arrival Routes;
7.   Standard Instrument Approach Procedures Charts;
8.   FAA Form 7233-4, ATC Flight Plan;
9.   Navigation Log/Flight Log;
10.   Load Manifest Form;
11.   Weight and Balance Form;
12.   Dispatch Release Form;
13.   Aeronautical Information Manual;
14.   Computer and Plotter;
15.   NOTAM Information;
16.   14 CFR parts 1, 25, 61, 65 Subpart C, 71, 91, 110, 119, 121, and 139;
17.   49 CFR parts 175, 830, and 1544;

18. Completed FAA Form 8400-3, Application for an Airman Certificate and/or Rating or IACRA application information;
19. Airman Knowledge Test Report;
20. Pilot Certificate (if applicable);
21. Statement of Graduation Certificate (if applicable);
22. Identification—Photo/Signature ID;
23. Notice of Disapproval/Letter of Discontinuance (if applicable); and
24. Examiner's Fee (if applicable).

**NOTE:** *If the applicant was trained in an FAA-approved dispatcher certification course, materials used in that course may be substituted for company specific materials supplied by the applicant.*

## Examiner[1] Responsibility

The examiner conducting the practical test is responsible for determining that the applicant meets the acceptable standards of knowledge and skill for each Task within the practical test standards. There is no formal division between the knowledge (oral) and skill (demonstration of abilities) portions of the practical test. The portion of this test devoted to manual flight planning may be considered a demonstration of skill; however, an examiner must test the applicant in his or her knowledge of the manual flight planning process and the calculations involved. Evaluation of applicants must be an ongoing process throughout the test. Oral questioning, to determine the applicant's knowledge of Tasks and related safety factors, should be used prudently at all times. Examiners shall test to the maximum extent practicable the applicant's correlative abilities, rather than rote memorization of facts, throughout the practical test.

An examiner should allot, on average, no less than 4 hours and no more than 6 hours to conduct a test.

In accordance with the requirements of 14 CFR 65.53(b)(2) and ICAO English Language proficiency requirements, the examiner must conduct the test and application process entirely in the English language. The English language component of crew coordination and communication skills can never be in doubt for the satisfactory outcome of the test. Normal restatement of questions as would be done for a native English speaking applicant is still permitted and is **not** grounds for disqualification.

If the examiner determines that a Task is incomplete or the outcome is uncertain, the examiner may require the applicant to repeat that

---

[1] The word "examiner" is used throughout these standards to denote either a qualified FAA inspector or FAA-designated examiner who conducts the official practical test.

Task, or portions of that Task. This provision has been made in the interest of fairness and does not mean that instruction, practice, or the repetition of an unsatisfactory Task is permitted any time during the test. When practical, the remaining Tasks of the practical test phase should be completed before repeating the questionable Task.

**NOTE:** *Where appropriate, the applicant should be allowed to use printed reference material commonly available to an aircraft dispatcher while on duty.*

## Satisfactory Performance

Satisfactory performance to meet the requirements for certification is based on the applicant's ability to:

1. perform the Tasks specified in the Areas of Operation within the approved standards outlined in this test book and the aircraft performance capabilities and limitations;
2. follow normal, abnormal, and emergency procedures as required by the regulations and company procedures;
3. demonstrate sound judgment, aeronautical decision-making, and dispatch resource management skills; and
4. apply aeronautical knowledge.

"Satisfactory performance" means that, in the judgment of the examiner, the applicant is able to demonstrate skill and correctly respond to the examiner's questions at least 70 percent of the time. Each examiner must have a method for making this determination.

## Unsatisfactory Performance

If, in the judgment of the examiner, the applicant does not meet the objective of performance of any Task performed, the associated Area of Operation is failed and; therefore, the practical test is failed.

The examiner or applicant may discontinue the test at any time when the failure of an Area of Operation makes the applicant ineligible for the certificate sought. *The test may be continued only with the consent of the applicant.* If the test is discontinued, the applicant is entitled to credit for only those Areas of Operation and their associated Tasks satisfactorily performed. However, during the re-test and at the discretion of the examiner, any Task may be re-evaluated, including those previously passed.

Errors, lack of performance and/or failures in any area should be considered as grounds for failure of the entire Aircraft Dispatcher Practical Test. Typical areas of unsatisfactory performance and grounds for disqualification are:

- Failure to appropriately apply conditions and limitations of any minimum equipment list (MEL)/Configuration Deviation List (CDL) item;

- Actions by the applicant that would constitute a violation of the Code of Federal Regulations (CFRs) if the applicant were actually dispatching a flight;

- Exceeding any Airplane Flight Manual (AFM) limitation;

- Failure to comply with operation specifications (OpSpecs);

- Failure to properly interpret weather information; and

- Failure to properly interpret any Notice to Airmen (NOTAMS).

### Notice of Disapproval

When a Notice of Disapproval is issued, the examiner shall record the applicant's unsatisfactory performance in terms of the Area of Operation and specific Task(s) not meeting the standard appropriate to practical test conducted. The Area(s) of Operation/Task(s) not tested and the number of practical test failures shall also be recorded.

### Letter of Discontinuance

When a practical test is discontinued for reasons other than unsatisfactory performance (e.g., equipment failure or illness), FAA Form 8400-3, Application for an Airman Certificate and/or Rating, and, if applicable, the Airman Knowledge Test Report, shall be returned to the applicant. The examiner at that time shall prepare, sign, and issue a Letter of Discontinuance to the applicant. The Letter of Discontinuance shall identify the Areas of Operation and their associated Tasks of the practical test that were successfully completed. The applicant shall be advised that the Letter of Discontinuance shall be presented to the examiner when the practical test is resumed, and made part of the certification file.

### Dispatch Resource Management (DRM)

The NTSB has found that inadequate operational control and inadequate collaborative decision-making have been contributing factors in air carrier accidents. Effective management of available resources by aircraft dispatchers is one essential deterrent to such accidents. In exercising operational control, the aircraft dispatcher coordinates with flight crewmembers, air traffic controllers (ATC), and other members of a vast team in order to meet the requirements of daily flight operations. AC 121-32, Dispatch Resource Management Training, encourages the aircraft dispatcher's knowledge of the functions of the other participants throughout the operation environment. Two expected benefits to the aircraft dispatcher are: (1) better handling of information that affects the safety of flight operations; and (2) a better interface with each pilot in command, consistent with the joint responsibility requirement outlined in 14 CFR part 121.

Examiners are required to exercise proper DRM competencies in conducting tests, as well as expecting the same from applicants.

## *Aeronautical Decision Making and Risk Management*

The examiner shall evaluate the applicant's ability throughout the practical test to use good aeronautical decision-making procedures in order to evaluate risks. The examiner shall accomplish this requirement by developing scenarios that incorporate as many Tasks as possible to evaluate the applicant's risk management skills in making safe aeronautical decisions. For example, the examiner may develop a scenario that incorporates weather decisions and performance planning. The applicant's ability to utilize all the assets available in making a risk analysis to determine the safest course of action is essential for satisfactory performance. The scenarios should be realistic and within the capabilities of the aircraft and company operations used for the practical test.

*(this page intentionally left blank)*

# Areas of Operation

## I. Flight Planning/Dispatch Release

### Task A: Regulatory Requirements

References:  14 CFR parts 1, 25, 61, 65 subpart C and Appendix A,
14 CFR parts 71, 91, 121, and 139; 49 CFR parts 175,
830, and 1544; AC 61-84, AC 90-105; AC 91-70;
General Operations Manual; Operations
Specifications.

NOTE:  Where appropriate, questions on other Areas of Operation
may be based on the assigned flight.

Objective:  To determine the applicant:

1. Can explain the regulatory requirements for obtaining an
   aircraft dispatcher certificate and discuss why air carriers
   employ dispatchers.
2. Exhibits adequate knowledge of the elements of flight
   planning and dispatch release(s) by preparing a flight plan,
   load manifest, take off data information, and dispatch
   release for a flight between designated airports.
3. Is able to plan the flight in accordance with regulatory
   requirements, operations specifications, and company
   procedures and provide all required information for that
   flight to the PIC.
4. Can recognize additional information that may affect the
   safety of the flight during flight and provide that information
   to the PIC in a timely manner.

### Task B: Meteorology

References:  14 CFR part 65 subpart C and Appendix A and 14
CFR part 121; FAA-H-8083-25; AC 00-6, AC 00-45;
AIM.

Objective:  To determine, through oral questioning and the flight
plan/dispatch release exercise, the applicant:

1. Understands and can explain elements of basic weather
   studies and weather theory, such as the Earth's motion and
   its effects on weather.
2. Demonstrates adequate knowledge of regional and local
   weather types, structures and characteristics of the

atmosphere, application and briefing of the flight plan/dispatch release exercise, including—

a. Pressure.
b. Wind.
c. Clouds.
d. Fog.
e. Ice.
f. Air masses.
g. Fronts.

## Task C: *Weather Observations, Analysis, and Forecasts*

References: *14 CFR part 65 subpart C and Appendix A and 14 CFR part 121; FAA-H-8083-25; AC 00-6, AC 00-45, AC 91-51, AC 120-60, AC 120-117; AIM.*

**NOTE:** *Where current weather reports, forecasts, or other pertinent information are not available, this information shall be simulated by the examiner in a manner that adequately measures the applicant's competence. Examples of aviation weather information are indicated within parentheses below, as appropriate.*

**Objective:** To determine, through oral questioning and the flight plan/dispatch release exercise, the applicant:

1. Exhibits adequate knowledge of the elements of aviation weather information by obtaining, reading, and analyzing the applicable items, such as—

   a. Aviation weather reports and forecasts (ATIS, METAR, SPECI, TAF, FA, FB, CWSU, MIS, GTG-2, CWA, WH, AC, WW, AWW).
   b. Pilot and radar reports (PIREPS, SD, satellite weather imagery, RADATs).
   c. Surface analysis charts.
   d. Significant weather prognostic charts (SIG WX).
   e. Winds and temperatures aloft (FB).
   f. Freezing level charts (FB, RADATs, FA, surface analysis chart, constant pressure charts).
   g. Composite moisture stability charts.
   h. Weather depiction charts.
   i. Constant pressure analysis charts.
   j. Tables and conversion graphs.
   k. Aviation Hazard forecasts, notices and advisories such as: SIGMETs, AIRMETs (WS, WA, WST), Volcanic Ash Advisory Statement, and Volcanic Ash forecast Transport and Dispersion Chart (VAAS, and VAFTAD).

l. Field condition reports.
m. NOTAMs/NOTAM systems.
n. EWINS (enhanced weather information system).

2. Correctly analyzes the assembled weather information pertaining to the proposed route of flight and destination airport, and determines whether an alternate airport is required and properly briefs the examiner. If an alternate is required, determines whether the selected alternate meets the requirements of the CFRs and the operations specifications.

## Task D:  *Weather-Related Hazards*

References:  *FAA-H-8083-15, FAA-H-8083-25; AC 00-6, AC 00-45, AC 20-29, AC 20-117, AC 91-43, AC 91-74; Airplane Flight Manual, General Operations Manual, Operations Manuals.*

Objective:  To determine that the applicant demonstrates adequate knowledge of the elements of weather hazards by applying all appropriate performance penalties and corrections on the manual flight plan/dispatch release and then appropriately briefing or discussing with the examiner weather hazards, such as:

1. Crosswinds and gusts.
2. Contaminated runways.
3. Restrictions to surface visibility.
4. Turbulence and wind shear.
5. Icing.
6. Thunderstorms and microbursts.
7. Tornadoes.
8. Hurricanes.
9. Typhoons.
10. Volcanic ash.

## Task E:  *Aircraft Systems, Performance, and Limitations*

References:  *14 CFR part 65 subpart C and Appendix A and 14 CFR part 121; Airplane Flight Manual; Operations Manuals; MEL/CDL; FAA-H-8083-1; AC 120-27.*

**Objective:** To determine the applicant:

1. Exhibits adequate knowledge of the principles of flight for group I and group II aircraft, and the elements of performance limitations, including thorough knowledge of the adverse effects of exceeding any limitation.
2. Demonstrates proficient use and knowledge of appropriate aircraft performance charts, tables, graphs, or other data relating to such items as—

   a. Accelerate-stop distance.
   b. Accelerate-go distance.
   c. Takeoff performance—all engines, and engine(s) inoperative.
   d. Climb performance,—all engines, and engine(s) inoperative.
   e. Service ceiling; all engines, and engine(s) inoperative.
   f. Cruise performance.
   g. Fuel consumption, range, and endurance.
   h. Descent performance.
   i. Go-around from rejected landing.
   j. Landing performance.
   k. Quick turnaround performance.
   l. Drift down.

3. Describes appropriate aircraft performance airspeeds used during specific phases of flight.
4. Describes the effects of meteorological conditions upon performance characteristics and correctly applies these factors to a specific chart, graph, or other performance data.
5. Computes the center-of-gravity location for a specific load condition (as specified by the examiner), including adding, removing, and shifting weight.
6. Determines that the takeoff weight, landing weight, and zero fuel weight are within limits.
7. Describes economics of flight procedures, including performance and fuel tankering.
8. Demonstrates good planning and knowledge of procedures in applying operational factors affecting aircraft performance.
9. Demonstrates and applies, using correct terminology, adequate aircraft systems knowledge related to—

   a. Flight controls.
   b. Autoflight.
   c. Hydraulics.
   d. Electrical.
   e. Air conditioning and pressurization.

f. Ice and rain protection.
g. Avionics, communication and navigation.
h. Powerplants and auxiliary power units.
i. Fuel systems and sources.
j. Oil system.
k. Landing gear and brakes.
l. Fire detection and protection.
m. Emergency and abnormal procedures.
n. Minimum equipment list (MEL)/configuration deviation list (CDL).

## Task F: Navigation and Aircraft Navigation Systems

References:  14 CFR part 65 subpart C and Appendix A and 14 CFR part 121; Airplane Flight Manual, General Operations Manual; AIM.

Objective:  To determine the applicant demonstrates adequate knowledge of navigation and aircraft navigation equipment and procedures, such as:

1. Navigation charts, symbols, and the national airspace system.
2. Airborne navigation instruments and automated databank systems—

   a. Electronic flight instrument system (EFIS).
   b. Flight management system (FMS).

3. Special navigation operations and performance—

   a. RVSM/DRVSM (Reduced Vertical Separation Minimums/Domestic Reduced Vertical Separation Minimums).
   b. ETOPS (Extended Operations).
   c. RNP (Required Navigation Performance).
   d. RNAV routes (Area Navigation).

      i. GNSS (Global Navigation Satellite System).

         (1) WAAS (Wide Area Augmentation System) and GPS (Global Positioning System).

      ii. Inertial Based Systems.

   e. FMS (Flight Management System).

4. Navigation definitions, time references and location (0° longitude, UTC).
5. Navigation systems including—

a. VHF Omnidirectional Range (VOR).
b. Distance Measuring Equipment (DME).
c. Instrument Landing System (ILS).
d. Marker Beacon Receiver/Indications.
e. Transponder/Altitude Encoding.
f. Automatic Direction Finding (ADF).
g. Long Range Navigation (LORAN).
h. Inertial Navigation System (INS).
i. Inertial Reference System (IRS).
j. Radio Area Navigation (RNAV).
k. Doppler Radar.
l. Global Positioning System (GPS).

## Task G: Practical Dispatch Applications

References: 14 CFR part 65 subpart C and Appendix A; AC 60-22, AC 121-32.

Objective: To determine the applicant exhibits adequate knowledge, judgment, and authority to influence and prevent aircraft accidents/incidents through knowledge of the following elements:

1. DRM (dispatcher resource management) procedures.
2. Human factors, teamwork, communications, and information exchange.
3. Aeronautical decision-making.
4. Situational awareness, assessment, and problem solving.
5. Generation and evaluation of alternatives.
6. Contingency planning.
7. Human error and technology-induced error.
8. Support tools and technologies.
9. Tradeoffs and prioritization.
10. Individual and organizational factors.
11. Prevention, detection, and recovery from errors.
12. Company risk management procedures, as appropriate.

## Task H: Manuals, Handbooks, and Other Written Guidance

References: 14 CFR part 65 subpart C and Appendix A and 14 CFR part 121; 49 CFR parts 175, 830, and 1544; General Operations Manual, Operations Specifications, MEL/CDL, Airplane Flight Manual; FAA-H-8083-25, FAA-H-8261-1; AC 00-2, AC 91-70, AC 90-91, AC 90-105, AC 121-26; FAA Order 7340.2, FAA Order 8260.3; Operations Manuals, AIM/IFIM.

Objective: To determine the applicant demonstrates adequate knowledge of and can effectively locate the appropriate manuals, handbooks, and other resource materials required for dispatching aircraft and to accomplish the Tasks in the practical test guide, such as:

1. 14 CFR part 65.
2. 14 CFR part 121.
3. 49 CFR part 175.
4. 49 CFR part 830.
5. 49 CFR part 1544.
6. General Operating Manual.
7. Operations Specifications.

## II.    Preflight, Takeoff, and Departure

### Task A:    Air Traffic Control Procedures

*References:*    *14 CFR part 65 subpart C and Appendix A, 14 CFR parts 91 and 121; FAA-H-8261-1; AIM/IFIM.*

**Objective:**    To determine the applicant exhibits adequate knowledge of the elements of air traffic control, including:

1. ATC responsibilities.
2. ATC facilities and equipment.
3. Airspace classification and route structure.
4. FAA Form 7233-4 flight plans and codes.
5. ATC separation minimums.
6. ATC flow control.
7. ATC traffic management.
8. ATC communications, protocol, and regulations.
9. Voice and data link communications.
10. DP/SID/ODP/RNAV (Departure procedure, standard instrument departure, obstacle departure procedure, area navigation).
11. Area Departures.
12. Terminal area charts, en route low/high charts.
13. Approved departure procedures and takeoff minimums.
14. Abnormal procedures.

### Task B:    Airports, Crew, and Company Procedures

*References:*    *14 CFR parts 117 and 121; General Operations Manual, Operations Specifications, A/FD; En Route High/low Charts, Terminal Area Charts; SIDs.*

**Objective:**    To determine the applicant demonstrates adequate knowledge in the elements of airport operations, crew requirements and company procedures, such as:

1. Crew qualifications and limitations.
2. Dispatch area, routes, and main terminals.
3. Airport diagrams, charts, and symbols.
4. Authorization of flight departure with concurrence of pilot in command.
5. Company approved departure procedures.
6. Airport/facility directory.
7. Takeoff alternate.

## III.    Inflight Procedures

### Task A:    Routing, Re-Routing, and Flight Plan Filing

*References:*    *14 CFR parts 91 and 121; AIM; FAA-H-8083-15;*
*Airport Facility Directory; General Operations Manual,*
*Operations Specifications.*

**Objective:**    To determine the applicant demonstrates adequate
knowledge of and skill to apply the following elements:

1.    ATC routing.
2.    ATC re-routing and company and crew communication
requirements.
3.    Re-filing of ATC Flight Plan.
4.    Canceling of ATC Flight Plan.
5.    Amended release procedures.
6.    Inflight diversions.
7.    Intermediate stops.
8.    Alternate procedures.
9.    Refueling and provisional airports.
10.    Weather requirements for airports.

### Task B:    En Route Communication Procedures and
Requirements

*References:*    *14 CFR parts 91 and 121; General Operations*
*Manual, Operations Specifications.*

**Objective:**    To determine the applicant demonstrates adequate
knowledge of the elements and method of inflight
communications, such as:

1.    Voice and data link communication requirements.
2.    Company and ATC communications, protocol, and
regulations.
3.    Company and ATC position reports and requirements.
4.    Flight following.
5.    Aircraft communications addressing and reporting system
(ACARS).
6.    Selective Calling System (SELCAL).
7.    High frequency communications (HF).
8.    Very high frequency communications (VHF)
9.    Satellite communications (SATCOM).
10.    Controller Pilot Data Link Communications (CPDLC).

# IV. Arrival, Approach, and Landing Procedures

## Task: ATC and Air Navigation Procedures

*References: 14 CFR parts 91 and 121; Operations Specifications, General Operations Manual, AIM; FAA-H-8083-15, FAA-H-8261-1; AC 120-28, AC 120-29, AC 120-57.*

**Objective:** To determine the applicant exhibits adequate knowledge of:

1. Area arrivals.
2. Transition routes and procedures.
3. Standard terminal arrival routes (STARs).
4. Instrument approach procedures (IAPs) and charts.
5. Precision approach procedures.

    a. CAT I ILS.
    b. CAT II ILS.
    c. CAT III ILS.
    d. ILS PRM (Precision Runway Monitor).
    e. PAR approach (Precision Approach Radar).

6. Non-precision approach procedures.
7. ATC separation minimums.
8. ATC priority handling.

# V.    Post-Flight Procedures

## Task A:    *Communication Procedures and Requirements*

*References:*    *14 CFR parts 91 and 121; General Operations*
*Manual, AIM.*

**Objective:**    To determine the applicant exhibits adequate
knowledge of the elements of regulatory and company
post-flight communication procedures and required
company documents, such as:

1.    Arrival message components, requirements and
communication protocol.
2.    Normal and alternate methods of communications delivery.

## Task B:    *Flight Documentation*

*References:*    *14 CFR parts 91 and 121; General Operations*
*Manual.*

**Objective:**    To determine the applicant demonstrates adequate
knowledge of the elements of:

1.    Regulatory requirements and post flight disposition of the
dispatch release, weight and balance, load manifest,
weather documents, communications records, and other
flight documents and reports.

# VI.    Abnormal and Emergency Procedures

## *Task:    Abnormal and Emergency Procedures*

*References:    14 CFR parts 91 and 121; 49 CFR parts 175, 830, and 1544; General Operations Manual, Airplane Flight Manual, AIM.*

**Objective:**    To determine that the applicant exhibits adequate knowledge and proficiency in the elements abnormal and emergency procedures, such as:

1.    Security measures on the ground.
2.    Security measures in the air.
3.    FAA responsibility and services.
4.    Collection and dissemination of information on overdue or missing aircraft.
5.    Means of declaring an emergency.
6.    Responsibility for declaring an emergency.
7.    Required reporting of an emergency.
8.    NTSB reporting requirements.
9.    49 CFR part 1544 requirements.